The Fearless Banker

Banking Case Studies and Rationale

Unlock Proven Strategies and Practical Insights to Tackle Everyday Banking Dilemmas, Achieve Excellence in Credit Decisions and Become an Extraordinary Banking Professional!

Volume - 1

Kumar Gaurav Khullar
(Ex-Bank of India, Ex- Punjab & Sind Bank)
(MBA-Indian Institute of Management, Raipur,
MCA, Centre for Development of Advanced Computing,
CDAC Noida)

INDIA · SINGAPORE · MALAYSIA

This book has been published with all efforts taken to make the material error-free after the consent of the author. However, the author and the publisher do not assume and hereby disclaim any liability to any party for any loss, damage, or disruption caused by errors or omissions, whether such errors or omissions result from negligence, accident, or any other cause.

While every effort has been made to avoid any mistake or omission, this publication is being sold on the condition and understanding that neither the author nor the publishers or printers would be liable in any manner to any person by reason of any mistake or omission in this publication or for any action taken or omitted to be taken or advice rendered or accepted on the basis of this work. For any defect in printing or binding the publishers will be liable only to replace the defective copy by another copy of this work then available.

DEDICATION

To my beloved mother, Smt. Punam, whose strength and unwavering love shaped my destiny. Single-handedly, she nurtured and educated me after losing my father when I was barely two, becoming my greatest inspiration and role model.

To my dear wife Tanu, whose faith in me ignited the courage to leave the comfort of a 9-to-5 banking job to follow my passion for Writing, Teaching and Research. Your unwavering support made this journey possible.

To my wonderful daughters, Pavi and Udyati—your laughter and love are my greatest comfort. No matter how hectic the day, you are my peace, my joy, and my deepest inspiration.

This book is for you.

CONTENTS

Preface

Why Do Some Bankers Struggle While Others Excel?

The answer isn't in textbooks. It lies in real-world experience, decision-making skills, and the ability to handle complex banking situations under pressure.

When I first stepped into the banking industry, brimming with enthusiasm and excitement, I soon realized a stark reality. There was a significant gap between the theoretical knowledge I had acquired and the practical scenarios that unfolded daily in the bank. Every day unraveled a different challenge, a complicated decision, and an unprecedented situation demanding an immediate solution.

Handling a garnishee order, tackling fraudulent collateral pledges, resolving nomination disputes, making credit decisions under ambiguity—these are just a few of the many real challenges that bankers face daily. Most professionals, especially newly promoted officers had to go through without proper preparation.

The truth is, in banking, your success isn't defined by how much you know, but by how well you apply that knowledge when it matters most. A single misstep can lead to audit red flags, financial losses, show-cause notices, or even career-threatening disciplinary actions. Many talented officers suffer this fate, not because they are not trying hard enough, but due to not being guided properly.

This Book Is the Mentor I Never Had!

When I entered the banking industry, I wished that I had a mentor or at least a book that would guide me through these real-life banking situations. Unfortunately, at that period, the majority of the resources available were heavy on theories and it was of little use when faced with practical problems.

That's why I wrote this book.

This book is not another theory-heavy banking manual. Rather, it is a compilation of 39 pragmatic case studies that embody the real-life challenges confronting bankers daily-special cases of credit risk, compliance, operational, legal, and customer disputes. Each case study comes with clear, actionable solutions to help you:

a)   Make better decisions in high-pressure situations.
b)   Avoid costly mistakes that can impact your career.
c)   Strengthen your reputation as a competent and confident banker.
d)   Master the art of handling internal audits, regulatory scrutiny, and risk assessment.
e)   Gain clarity on real-world dilemmas that often leave bankers confused and vulnerable.

This book will elevate your problem-solving skills, sharpen your judgment, and equip you with the expertise that top-performing bankers possess.

Who Is This Book for?

a)   Newly promoted officers who are taking on managerial roles without prior real-world exposure.
b)   Branch Managers, Credit Officers, and Banking Professionals who deal with operational, compliance, and credit-related challenges.
c)   Bankers preparing for promotion interviews who want to demonstrate sound decision-making skills.
d)   Anyone in the banking or finance sector who wants to accelerate their professional growth and minimize risk in their career.

Why This Book Matters Now More Than Ever?

The banking industry is evolving at an unprecedented pace. Regulatory oversight is getting tighter, fraud risks are rising, and digital banking has introduced new layers of complexity. Promotions are happening faster, often placing officers in key decision-making roles before they've had enough hands-on exposure.

This book will help quick learning and prepare you to lead in a world where application rather than knowledge is the differentiator for the success of the project.

Whether you are a new officer, a seasoned banker, or someone looking to future-proof your career, this book will transform you from an uncertain, hesitant banker into a decisive, confident, and highly skilled professional.

Get ready to empower yourself and become an expert in modern banking.

Read this book. Apply its lessons. Become the fearless banker others look up to.

Happy reading!
Kumar Gaurav Khullar
kumargauravkhullar1@gmail.com

How to Proceed with This Book?

I would like to congratulate you on beginning an exciting journey designed to deepen your knowledge, enhance your decision-making ability and improve your practical banking skills. Before you begin exploring the compelling scenarios and case studies laid out in the following chapters, allow me to share with you the optimal approach to deriving maximum benefit from this book.

I would like to emphasize that the case studies and scenarios contained in these pages are all drawn from real-life experiences in actual banking environments. They are recreated here only for educational purposes. All cases have been adapted, generalized and simplified for privacy, compliance and confidentiality. Therefore, any resemblance to specific individuals, institutions, banks, or branches is entirely coincidental. Any name, including that of banks, staff, customers and places, set out herein are purely hypothetical and used only for the purpose of illustrating practical situations.

The book has been structured into useful case studies taken from day-to-day banking operations, compliance issues, customer management, credit appraisal, risk management, digital banking and many more. Each case situation illustrates a commonplace yet delicate situation in which banking professionals frequently find themselves, more so with those new to banking or stepping up to more responsible and senior roles.

To get the most from this book, I recommend the following structured approach.

1)**Active Reading:** Approach each chapter with active engagement. Imagine yourself put into the situations described. Pause frequently for reflection. Ask yourself what you would have done in that situation. As you immerse yourself in every scenario, you will learn some useful lessons and develop your problem-solving skills.

2) **Critical Thinking and Analysis:** Each case concludes with a detailed analysis and discussion of the scenario, highlighting critical learnings, suggested solutions, common mistakes, best practices, and practical tips. While reading these, compare your initial evaluation and decision with the analysis provided.

Such reflection fosters a deeper understanding and reinforces crucial banking principles.

3) Continuous Learning: Banking today is more challenging than ever, with increased digitization, stringent regulatory oversight, and rising compliance risks. Be sure to take a good look at chapters that relate directly to digital banking, regulatory guidelines, audits, and grievance handling. This will help you stay one step ahead and deal more easily with challenges.

4) Discussion and Debate: Wherever possible, discuss these scenarios with colleagues, peers, or study groups. Sometimes different opinions and discussions can throw up new insights. This will help you remain proactive.

5) Supplementary Reference: You may frequently revisit case studies that resonate most deeply with your personal experiences or professional aspirations. Every time you look, you will discover something new to help your ongoing professional development.

Finally, remember that the real aim of this book extends far beyond theoretical knowledge; it aims to build within you a robust practical approach to real-world banking. Its ultimate purpose is to prepare you to manage scenarios proactively, confidently, and ethically—equipping you to handle daily challenges efficiently while reducing the chances of errors that may result in avoidable stress, suspensions, or regulatory penalties.

Approach this book with curiosity and openness. As you embark upon the learning process, allow yourself to learn, unlearn and relearn. May these practical situations instill in you a passion and conviction which would help you be a more thoughtful, responsible and able banking professional.

Let's begin this transformative journey!

Case Study 1

The Garnishee Order Dilemma – A Bank's Legal and Ethical Balancing Act

Introduction

In the complex world of banking, compliance with legal directives while ensuring customer trust is a delicate balancing act. One such order is the Garnishee order. It is a court order issued under order 21, rule 46 of the Civil Procedure Code attaching the funds of the judgment debtor which are held by any 3rd party, including banks. This case study explores a practical scenario where a bank faced significant challenges in implementing a garnishee order while navigating regulatory compliances and customer grievances.

The Scenario

Your bank received a garnishee order against one of your customers, Mr. Ramesh Verma, a prominent businessman. The order was issued by a district court in favor of Amarjyothi Enterprises, a creditor who had won a legal suit against Verma for non-payment of dues amounting to ₹25 lakhs. The order directed the bank to freeze the available balance in Verma's account & remit the amount to the court upon confirmation.

At the time of receiving the order, Verma had multiple accounts with the bank, including a savings account with ₹5 lakh, a current account with ₹10 lakh, & a fixed deposit of ₹15 lakh. The bank now faced several legal & operational challenges in executing the garnishee order while adhering to banking regulations.

Problem Statement

The primary concerns of the bank were:

1) **Identifying the Attachability of Funds**: Should the bank freeze only the savings & current account balances, or should the fixed deposit also be considered?

2) **Handling Joint Accounts and Other Liabilities**: If Verma had joint accounts, could the garnishee order extend to those?

3) **Processing Unclear Credits and Future Transactions**: Should the bank attach incoming funds that were deposited after the order was received?

4) **Balancing Customer Rights with Legal Obligations**: How should the bank proceed if Verma did challenge the order or ask for modifications?

Detailed Analysis & Solution

1) Order NISI vs. Order Absolute – The Bank's First Step in Compliance

When your bank received the garnishee order against Mr. Ramesh Verma, the first step was to determine its legal standing. Garnishee orders are issued in two stages as per the Civil Procedure Code, Order 21, Rule 46:

a) **Order NISI (Provisional Order)** – A preliminary order where the bank is directed to freeze the account but not remit the funds immediately. This allows the judgment debtor (Verma) an opportunity to present objections, if any, before the court.

b) **Order Absolute (Final Order)** – If the court finds no valid objections or overrules them, it converts the Order NISI into Order Absolute, directing the bank to transfer the attached funds to the court or creditor.

Following legal protocol, the Bank immediately recorded the date & time of receipt of the Order NISI in its system & froze Verma's available balances in his savings and current accounts (₹15 lakhs total). The bank also informed Verma about the legal restriction, allowing him to contest the order if necessary.

Additionally, all cheques issued by Verma after the garnishee order was returned with the remark "Refer to Drawer", ensuring compliance with the directive. The legal and compliance team of the bank was closely observing the situation and waiting for the court directions regarding the final remittance.

2) Handling Fixed Deposits and Right of Set-Off – A Crucial Banking Decision

One of the major concerns for the bank while executing the garnishee order against Mr. Ramesh Verma was whether his fixed deposit (FD) of ₹15 lakh should be attached. According to banking regulations, a garnishee order applies only to available balances in a debtor's account at the time of order receipt. However, the situation becomes complex when the customer has a fixed deposit, especially if there is a lien or right of set-off involved.

Legal Considerations

a)   If Verma had availed a loan against his fixed deposit & a lien was marked, the bank's right of set-off would take precedence over the garnishee order. In such a case, the garnishee order would not apply to the FD.

b)   If no lien was marked & the fixed deposit was freely available, the bank sought court clarification before proceeding with the attachment.

Bank's Action

The Bank temporarily excluded the FD from the attachment, freezing only the savings & current account balances. However, it notified the court & awaited specific instructions regarding the FD. If the court explicitly included the FD in the final Order Absolute, the bank would have to liquidate it & remit the funds accordingly.

This approach of the bank ensured that the bank was legally compliant as well as to protect it from any disputes.

3) Joint Accounts and Trust Accounts – Addressing Complex Ownership Structures

While executing the garnishee order against Mr. Ramesh Verma, the bank faced a challenge in determining whether joint accounts & trust accounts held by Verma could be attached. The bank needed to make sure they only froze Verma's funds that were legally attachable and no other account holders' rights were violated.

Joint Accounts: Attachability Based on Ownership Structure

a)   If Verma held a joint account with his wife or business partner under the 'Either or Survivor' mandate, the garnishee order would not automatically apply. Because ownership in such accounts is shared, attaching the funds will affect the other account holder's rights.

b)   However, if the order explicitly named the joint account, the bank would be bound to attach the portion belonging to Verma. The court would have to step in when ownership percentages were unclear.

Trust Accounts: An Important Exemption

a) If Verma deposited money as trustee or fiduciary, the money legally belonged to beneficiaries and not to Verma. Hence, the garnishee order could not attach such accounts.

b) The Bank carefully examined the mandates and trust deeds related to the accounts before executing the order so that it may not create any wrongful attachment of the funds.

By closely studying ownership structures, the bank made sure it adhered to legal guidelines & avoided unnecessary disputes with co-account holders.

4) Uncleared Cheques and Future Credits – Addressing Dynamic Account Movements

One of the biggest operational challenges the bank faced while executing the garnishee order against Mr. Ramesh Verma was determining whether uncleared cheques & future credits could be attached. The bank had to ensure it only froze amounts legally due at the time of order receipt while complying with judicial directives.

Uncleared Cheques – Should They Be Considered?

a) If the garnishee order was received after a cheque had already been debited from Verma's account but before the cash was withdrawn, the bank's best course of action was to reject the cheque payment and mark it as "Refer to Drawer". This prevented wrongful disbursement of funds.

b) However, if the cheque was still in clearing & had not yet been debited, the bank was required to return the cheque unpaid to avoid violation of the order.

Future Credits – Are They Attachable?

a) The garnishee order applies only to the balance available at the time of order receipt. Any funds deposited into Verma's account after the order were not subject to attachment.

b) If there was an agreement to withdraw unrealized credits, such amounts can be attached legally.

To ensure compliance, the Bank closely monitored Verma's account transactions, rejecting unauthorized payments while segregating future credits from the attachment. This careful execution protected both the bank's legal standing & customer interests.

5) Remittance and Compliance – Ensuring Legally Sound Execution

After the NISI Order turned into an Order Absolute, the bank had to ensure complete legal compliance by sending the attached funds to the court and/or the creditor, as the case may be. This final step required meticulous verification & adherence to banking regulations to avoid legal repercussions.

Step-by-Step Compliance Process

1) Confirmation of Order Absolute

a)   After the stipulated response period, if Verma failed to contest the order or the court rejected his objections, the Order NISI was converted into an Order Absolute.

b)   This meant that the Bank was now legally required to remit the frozen funds to the court for payment to Amarjyothi Enterprises.

2) Final Account Verification

a)   The compliance team of the bank re-verified the total attached balance before transferring the funds (₹15 lakhs in savings and current account).

b)   If any part of the balance was mistakenly unfrozen or wrongly deducted, corrective actions were taken.

3) Fund Transfer and Closure

a)   The bank transferred the amount that was attached to the court along with proper documentation for audit purposes & protection of legal rights.

b)   A final notification was sent to Verma, confirming the action & closing the garnishee proceedings on his accounts.

The bank followed a systematic process of remittance and adherence which ensured regulatory compliance, limited risk exposure and legal propriety. It set a precedent for the handling of future garnishee orders.

Key Lessons for Bankers

1) **Legal Compliance vs. Customer Interests** – Banks must adhere to garnishee orders cautiously and protect the rights of the customers, while keeping the process transparent.

2) **Thorough Due Diligence** – Understanding different account types, lien positions, & joint account regulations is critical in implementing such orders.

3) **Proper Documentation & Timely Action** – Recording the date & time of the order receipt and taking immediate action minimizes risks for the bank.

* * *

CASE STUDY 2

BEYOND A SINGLE HEIR: UNRAVELLING THE COMPLEXITIES OF SUCCESSIVE AND SIMULTANEOUS NOMINATIONS

Introduction

In 2024, a transformative amendment was introduced in India's banking sector to address a long-standing challenge i.e. managing nominee-related disputes in deposit accounts. In the past, depositors were only allowed to nominate one person, often resulting in legal and familial issues when the claim was settled. To modify these norms & streamline processes, the Reserve Bank of India (RBI) announced provisions for Multiple Nominees allowing up to four nominees with two new methods – Successive Nomination & Simultaneous Nomination. This case explores the policy's implementation, real-world implications, challenges faced by banks, & actionable solutions.

The Scenario

Meera Sharma, a 62-year-old retired government employee, opened a fixed deposit account of ₹10,23,456 with Sunshine Bank, a leading private sector bank in India. Worried about her wealth being divided equally among her four children Aakash, Bharat, Charu and Divya, she approaches her relationship manager for guidance

Under the new guidelines, Meera could choose between:

a) **Successive Nomination**: A priority-based approach where only one nominee has effective rights at any given time.

b) **Simultaneous Nomination**: A share-based method in which the nominees will receive specified proportions of deposit.

21

Problem Statement

Although the updated nomination framework makes it easier & clearer for depositors, it adds complications, both operationally & legally, such as:

a) Ensuring accuracy in nomination records.
b) Handling the possible disputes arising from incomplete/ invalid nominations.
c) Addressing procedural challenges when one or more nominees predecease the depositor.
d) Updating the banks' core banking systems to incorporate the same is a massive task.
e) Educating depositors & staff about the nuances of successive & simultaneous nominations.

Detailed Analysis

Successive Nomination: A Simplified Priority-Based Approach

Meera chose Successive Nomination prioritising her children in the below order:

1) Aakash (1st priority)
2) Bharat (2nd priority)
3) Charu (3rd priority)
4) Divya (4th priority)

This nomination method ensures that, at any point, only one nominee holds effective rights over the deposit. The key characteristics include:

a) **Priority Hierarchy:** If Aakash is alive, he will inherit the deposit entirely. If Aakash dies before Meera, then Bharat will take his heirs, followed by Charu and then Divya.
b) **Residual Risk:** If all nominees predecease the depositor, the deposit becomes unnominated, & the legal heirs would need to claim it as per the bank's deceased claim settlement policy.

Illustration of Events:

If Meera passes away on **March 15, 2025**, & Aakash survives her, the deposit of ₹10,23,456 will transfer solely to him. If Aakash passes away on **July 12, 2027**,

Bharat will become the effective nominee. If both Aakash & Bharat predecease Meera, Charu will inherit the deposit, and so forth.

This nomination method prevents quarrel among surviving nominees, but there should be proper documentation of the priority order in the banking CBS system.

Simultaneous Nomination: A Share-Based Approach

Alternatively, Meera would have gone for Simultaneous Nomination by splitting her deposit as under:

- Aakash: 30%
- Bharat: 25%
- Charu: 20%
- Divya: 25%

When Meera dies, the deposit will go to her children in these percentages. If any nominee dies before Meera, their portion would not be nominated & would therefore not be distributed.

Illustration of Events:

On Meera's death, the following scenarios could unfold:

a) Scenario 1 (All nominees alive):

Deposit of ₹10,23,456 distributed as:

- Aakash: ₹3,07,036.80
- Bharat: ₹2,55,864
- Charu: ₹2,04,691.20
- Divya: ₹2,55,864

b) Scenario 2 (Aakash predeceases Meera):

Remaining deposit of ₹10,23,456 distributed as:

- Bharat: ₹2,55,864
- Charu: ₹2,04,691.20
- Divya: ₹2,55,864

Invalid Nominations:

Should the percentages not equal to 100% (for example 30% Aakash, 25% Bharat, 20% Charu, 20% Divya), the nomination will be invalid and the deposit shall be treated as unnominated.

Comparison of Methods

Aspect	Successive Nomination	Simultaneous Nomination
Number of Nominees	Up to 4, with a defined priority order	Up to 4, with percentage-based shares
Distribution Mechanism	One nominee at a time	Simultaneous distribution
Flexibility	Limited	High
Complexity	Low	Moderate
Risk of Disputes	Minimal	Moderate

Challenges for Banks

1) Systemic Challenges:

    a)   Core banking systems must be upgraded to:

- Record up to four nominees.
- Support percentage calculations for simultaneous nominations.
- Handle succession mechanisms in successive nominations.

    b)   The estimated cost of system modification is ₹2.5–3 crore per mid-sized bank.

2) Dispute Resolution:

Simultaneous nominations may lead to disputes if:

    a)   Shares are unclear or incorrectly stated.

    b)   If the nominee dies before the depositor, then distribution of their share will be very difficult.

3) Operational Challenges:

    a)   Staff training is required to explain these changes to customers.

    b)   More documentation like updated nomination forms and customer acknowledgment slips.

4) Regulatory Compliance:

    a)   The amendments are in accordance with the provisions of Section 45ZA of the Banking Regulation Act, 1949 concerning nominee rights of depositors.

b)   As per the mandate of Reserve Bank of India (RBI), Banks should follow the latest guidelines and also convey the same at the time of inspection.

Actionable Steps for Banks

1) Customer Awareness Campaigns:

a)   Conduct workshops & seminars to educate customers about new nomination options.

b)   Help spread informative leaflets & Frequently Asked Questions (FAQs) at branches and on the internet.

2) Staff Training:

a)   Develop specialized training programs to equip staff with knowledge about successive & simultaneous nominations.

b)   Create quick reference guides for front-line employees.

3) Core Banking System Updates:

a)   Work with IT vendors so that necessary changes can be implemented into the system for compliance & automation of processes.

4) Dispute Management Framework:

Set up a strong dispute resolution system like the appointment of a nominee grievance officer.

Key Learnings for Bankers

1) Balancing Simplicity and Compliance: Banks must ensure that processes do not get complicated for customers while also remaining in accordance with law and regulations.

2) Educating Stakeholders: Continuous education of staff and customers is vital to minimizing errors & misunderstandings.

3) System Efficiency: To implement any policy changes it is important to have upgraded systems & automated solutions.

* * *

CASE STUDY 3

The Handwritten Scam: How Manipulated Fixed Deposits Led to an ₹88 Lakh Banking Fraud

Introduction

Maria D'Souza was a Senior Window Operator (SWO) at the Pernem Branch of Goenkar Bank, a mid-sized regional bank in Goa. Known for her polite demeanor & customer-centric approach, she had been with the branch for over 12 years. Due to her consistency & strong relationship with the customers, she was very trustworthy, especially in a rural setting where most of the customers were not financially literate.

However, this trust was betrayed when one morning, while she was absent, a regular customer John Rodrigues approached the Branch Manager Mr. Ravi Naik & requested the withdrawal of ₹1,42,750 from his Fixed Deposit (FD). John gave his original FD Receipt (FDR) as evidence for the deposit. When verified in the Bank's Core Banking System (CBS), Mr. Naik found that the account had only ₹45,320. Sensing something amiss, he initiated an investigation that unraveled a shocking pattern of fraud perpetrated by Maria, affecting several unsuspecting customers.

The Scenario

With the investigation the following irregularities & details came to light:

a) The FD receipt given to John was handwritten which is against the operational instructions of Goenkar Bank which instructs system-generated receipts.

b) The FDR amount had been altered from ₹45,320 to ₹1,42,750, both in words & figures. The alteration was subtle & strategically done, so it could not be detected in the normal checks.

c) John had deposited ₹1,42,750 with Maria in good faith & received the manipulated receipt. He was unaware of the discrepancy between the CBS record & the physical receipt.

d) The Branch Manager & another officer had verified & signed the original FDR for ₹45,320, but Maria had subsequently altered it before handing it over to the customer.

e) After investigation, the bank found that Maria had used the same method to defraud to the tune of ₹88,46,370 from over 56 customers in the last six-year period.

The fraudulent activities were facilitated by systemic & procedural gaps, such as:

a) **Mobile Number Gaps**: Nearly 68% of customers at the Pernem Branch did not have updated mobile numbers in the CBS, meaning no transaction alerts were sent.

b) **Lack of Monitoring**: Mandatory leave policies & job rotation guidelines were ignored. Maria had not availed a single day of leave in the last 22 months.

c) **Language Barriers**: Most of the customers were Konkani-speaking locals who did not approach higher officials for help due to apprehension of language & culture.

d) **Over-Familiarity**: Due to Maria's long-time tenure at the branch, colleagues & customers never challenged her behavior or her actions.

Problem Statement

How did the failure to enforce internal controls & monitoring mechanisms enable Maria to manipulate deposit operations, resulting in the loss of customer trust and financial fraud? What corrective measures can Goenkar Bank implement to prevent such incidents?

Detailed Analysis and Solution

Investigations revealed that fraud was orchestrated by many procedural lapses & weaknesses in internal systems, which were identified. The analysis & corresponding solutions are outlined below:

1) Procedural Violations

Findings:

Maria used to often issue handwritten FDRs instead of system-generated ones. She intentionally changed the amount of deposit in this case from ₹45,320 to ₹1,42,750. Similar discrepancies were observed across other accounts as well.

Solution:

a)   Mandatory system-generated receipts for all Fixed Deposit transactions.
b)   Conduct audits every three months to adhere to this policy.
c)   Use of barcode enabled FDR directly linked with CBS to remove the scope of manual tampering.

2) Lack of Customer Alerts

Findings:

Out of 2,358 active customers at the Pernem Branch, 1,607 (68.16%) had outdated or unregistered mobile numbers in the CBS. This left customers in the dark with their transactions & account overview.

Solution:

a)   Start a customer outreach process to collect the updated contact details. It is possible to incentivize this with small gifts or a fee waiver to complete KYC updating.
b)   Mandate that all deposits & withdrawals trigger SMS/email alerts.
c)   Create a new "Customer Alert Monitoring Dashboard" for the respective Branch staff to identify and follow up on accounts without updated contact numbers.

3) Job Rotation and Leave Policies

Findings:

Maria had not availed leave for 22 months, & the job rotation policy was not implemented on the ground. Just a yearly job rotation certificate was sent to the regional/Zonal Office. Because she had been continuously present, she manipulated the accounts with ease & without anyone's suspicion.

Solution:

a) Implement a mandatory job rotation policy audit, requiring RO/ZO staff to do surprise checks of branches and ensure staff to switch roles or branches every 2–3 years.
b) Make all staff take at least 5 consecutive days leave & make this mandatory for every staff member. This provides an opportunity to review their work in their absence.
c) Create a 'work shadowing system' where one employee cross-checks the other's work.

4) Supervisor Oversight

Findings:

FDRs were regularly signed by the Branch Manager & another officer without cross-verification of the physical receipt with CBS. This negligence allowed Maria to operate undetected.

Solution:

a) Supervisors should be trained on how to detect fraud, especially on how to handle physical documents.
b) Impose two-level authorization on FD creation and amendment.
c) Add the AI based fraud detection tools to the CBS to mark anomalies in real time.

5) Language Barriers

Findings:

Most customers at the Pernem Branch spoke Konkani while senior officers used to communicate in English or Hindi. Customers did not report discrepancies because of this linguistic barrier.

Solution:

a) Recruit multi-lingual staff proficient in Konkani, English, & Hindi.
b) Conduct workshops for existing staff to learn basic conversational Konkani.
c) Set up a dedicated grievance desk with interpreters for customer support.

Legal and HR Actions

Actions Against Maria

a) Maria was immediately suspended & later dismissed after the investigation.

b) An FIR was filed under Section 420 (Cheating and Dishonesty) & Section 468 (Forgery for Purpose of Cheating) of the Indian Penal Code (IPC).

c) A total of ₹22,14,630 was recovered from her terminal benefits. Maria is currently absconding, & her assets have been attached under court orders.

HR Measures

d) The HR department was instructed to perform compliance checks every year for leave & job rotation policy in all branches.

e) A comprehensive fraud awareness training programme was conducted for all staff.

Impact on Goenkar Bank

The fraud led to a temporary loss of customer trust & reputational damage for the bank. But, immediate corrective measures and open communication helped lessen the consequences. After compensating the affected customers, the bank has also enhanced its operational control to check the recurrence of such a case.

Key Learnings for Bankers

1) Internal Control Mechanisms Must Be Proactively Enforced

Most of the fraudulent activities can be attributed to the negligence of job rotations, leave policies, & customer alerts and other areas. Robust oversight mechanisms are essential.

2) Customer-Centric Communication Is Crucial

Regular transaction alerts, multilingual staff, & an approachable grievance system foster transparency and trust.

3) Technology as a Preventive Tool

AI-driven fraud detection systems and CBS-linked barcoded documents minimize manual errors & fraudulent practices.

* * *

When Partnerships Falter: A Deep Dive into Liability, Oversight, and Clayton's Rule

The Scenario

M/s R. K. Tobacco Industries is a partnership firm of three brothers namely, Arjun, Bhavesh and Chandan. The firm enjoys a well-maintained working capital limit of ₹25 lakhs. The facility was secured by way of an equitable mortgage over a factory building at a prime location. The Branch Manager (BM) often reviewed the account, which was seen as a model example of good conduct.

But things started to fall apart when Bhavesh planned to enter the booming construction business and set his sights on the factory property. Since the property showed immense potential for the establishment of a shopping complex, Bhavesh started urging the brothers to dissolve the partnership and partition the property. Through this, each of the partners would be in a position to exploit the property in the manner it suited best. His actions were resisted, which caused internal conflicts.

On October 4, 2024, the bank received a formal written notice from Bhavesh that he was no longer a partner of R. K. Tobacco Industries and he wanted to be released from his personal guarantee. Worried about the sudden event, the BM promptly froze the account and summoned the other partners for clarification.

Three days later, Arjun and Chandan told the BM that all differences had been sorted out and the partnership would continue uninterrupted. After getting an assurance the BM resumed the operation of the account but did not obtain a written withdrawal of the notice from Bhavesh.

On 20 April 2025, six months later from this incident, the BM is caught off-guard with a public notice in a newspaper. Bhavesh clearly stated that he had no connection with R K Tobacco Industries anymore, so he is also not responsible for its financial dealings. Baffled by the revelation, the BM reviewed the account and found a debit balance posted for ₹12 lakh, which raised critical questions about Bhavesh's liability and the bank's exposure.

Legal and Procedural Analysis

1) **The Crystallization of Liability:** Bhavesh's written notice in October 2024 legally notified his withdrawal from the partnership. Under Section 32 of Indian Partnership Act, 1932, a partner can retire by giving a notice where the partnership is at will. The bank should have regarded the partnership as dissolved as far as Bhavesh's liability is concerned, which would cease his liability from the date of receipt of the notice.

2) **Continuance of the Cash Credit Account:** By resuming the account operations again, without first obtaining written confirmation from all partners and/or making an amendment to the partnership the BM has exposed the bank to operational and legal risk. This mistake violates the prudent banking norms and Reserve Bank of India Master Directions on Bank Guarantee and Partnership accounts.

3) **Application of Clayton's Rule:** The Rules of Clayton's Case (Devaynes v. Noble, 1816) applies to the order of discharge of liabilities in a running account. Payments made into the account are deemed to settle the earliest debit first, unless you direct otherwise. To ascertain the balance of Bhavesh's liability, the account ledger must be examined from October 4, 2024. Payments made after the notice may have reduced or discharged his obligations entirely but can only be substantiated after detailed transactional analysis.

4) **Implications of Public Notice:** In April 2025, Bhavesh's advertisement made it clear that he is not connected with R K Tobacco Industries. Although this did not have any retrospective legal effect on the liability, it was reflective of a desire to withdraw, which may impact any legal proceedings related to disputes or outstanding debts.

5) **The Bank's Exposure:** The current outstanding amount of ₹12 lakhs is a risk for the bank. Any liability that arises after October 4, 2024, may no longer be attributable to Bhavesh. The Bank, accordingly, may recover the amount only from the other remaining partners or enforce the equitable mortgage.

Strategic Learnings for Bankers

1) **Enforce Procedural Rigor:**

   When a notice is received regarding the withdrawal of a partner from the firm, it is the duty of the bank to obtain an immediate joint declaration from all partners of the firm regarding the existence of the firm and the distribution of liabilities. Updated loan documents and guarantees should be added to this.

2) **Monitor Legal Notifications:**

   Notices, whether internal (e.g., partner communication) or external (e.g., public advertisements), should trigger a comprehensive review of account operations and legal compliance.

3) **Strengthen Risk Management:**

   Knowledge of Clayton's Rule and the relevant sections of the Indian Partnership Act, 1932 helps in proper valuation of and appropriate controlling of liability risk in partnership accounts.

Conclusion

This case shows how important it is to keep proper records, act quickly, and keep all legalities in mind for partnership accounts. By not obtaining a written withdrawal of the notice issued by Bhavesh, the BM made the bank vulnerable to disputes and recovery issues. A more proactive approach, anchored in legal and procedural diligence, could have safeguarded the bank's interests while ensuring compliance with regulatory norms.

* * *

DISCHARGED OR DECEIVED? THE HIGH-STAKES GAME OF ENDORSEMENT CANCELLATION

The Scenario: A Chain of Endorsements

Rajesh, the holder of a negotiable instrument – bill of exchange, comes into possession of a bill where Mohan is payee. The endorsements on the bill proceed as follows.

- First endorsement: Mohan (Payee)
- Second endorsement: Charan
- Third endorsement: Deepak
- Fourth endorsement: Esha

The endorsements made by Deepak and Charan are canceled by Rajesh intentionally. The key question is: **Does this action free Esha, the final endorser, from liability to Rajesh?**

Deep Dive into Legal Provisions

The **Negotiable Instruments Act, 1881,** addresses such scenarios under two critical sections:

1) **Section 40: Impairment of Endorser's Remedies**

   This section stipulates that when a holder of a negotiable instrument (here, Rajesh) destroys or impairs an endorser's remedies against prior parties without consent, the endorser is discharged from liability to the same extent as if the instrument had been paid at maturity.

2) **Section 39: Discharge by Cancellation of Signature**

   As per this section, a party liable on a negotiable instrument is discharged from liability if the holder intentionally cancels its signature. Cancellation should not be accidental but a deliberate act.

Application to the Case

When Rajesh cancels or strikes out Deepak and Charan's endorsements several legal principles come into play:

1) **Liability of Deepak and Charan:**

   By canceling their endorsements, Rajesh has directly discharged Deepak and Charan from liability. Under **Section 39**, this intentional cancellation will render their obligations under the bill null and void.

2) **Impact on Esha's Liability:**

   a) **Principal-Debtor-Surety Relationship:** Between Deepak and Esha, Deepak is the principal debtor and Esha is the surety. According to the established principles of suretyship, the surety shall be liable only when the principal debtor is liable.

   b) **Effect of Discharge:** By releasing Deepak (the main debtor) without Esha's approval, Rajesh has, according to Section 39, also released Esha. This concept works in conjunction with the concurrent liability doctrine of suretyship.

3) **Legal Position of Esha:**

   Rajesh, in order to enforce the liability against Esha, ought to have retained the liability of Deepak. As long as Deepak is not liable, Esha is absolved of liability as a surety cannot remain liable if the principal debtor is absolved.

Complex Interplay of Laws

Rajesh's act not only discharges the liability of the individual endorsers but also breaks the chain of liability of negotiable instruments. The trust on which the negotiable instrument system is built is violated along with the sanctity of the bill and it gives rise to many inventiveness. The impact goes beyond Esha, indicating a flaw in the procedural application of negotiable instruments.

Key Insights for Bankers

1) **Chain of Endorsements:** The chain of endorsement must be maintained for negotiable instruments to be enforceable. Any disturbance like cancellation without consent can discharge the parties from liability.

2) **Suretyship Dynamics:** Understanding the interplay between principal debtors and sureties is critical. If the principal debtor is discharged without the surety's consent, the instrument cannot be enforced against the surety.

3) **Holder's Responsibilities:** The holder is required to act within the limits set by law, failing which the instrument will be ineffective. If an endorser's right is impaired without due process, the instrument would be void.

Conclusion

Rajesh's cancellation of Deepak and Charan's endorsements discharged their liability and also discharged Esha from her liability as well. Rajesh's actions have made the instrument unenforceable against Esha. Subsequently, Rajesh cannot claim recovery from Esha under Sections 39 and 40 of the Negotiable Instruments Act, 1881.

* * *

CASE STUDY 6

LOAN APPROVED OR REJECTED? THE REAL IMPACT OF CIBIL SCORES ON BORROWERS

Introduction

Vijayawada City Bank (VCB), a reputed regional bank known for its prudent lending practices, is dedicated to helping customers meet their financial needs while maintaining asset quality. As a credit officer in the Vijayawada branch, you received five varied loan applications for appraisal recently. Each applicant had unique circumstances, CIBIL scores, and financial profiles. Figure out which loans can be sanctioned given the bank's risk management policies & also the regulatory framework given by the RBI.

The Scenario

The details of the five applicants are as follows:

Applicant Name	Loan Applied (₹)	CIBIL Score	Profession	Monthly Income (₹)	Key Financial Data
Mr. Cheteshwara Pujara	₹5,13,800	830	Government Servant	₹62,400	Steady income; well-maintained savings account with VCB.
Mr. Reddy Gopal	₹3,12,650	-1	Farmer	₹48,750 (Farm Income)	Regular farm income; consistent transactions in VCB account; no prior credit history.
Mr. Faiz Ahmed	₹2,04,250	580	Government Employee	₹40,320	Salary account with VCB; low CIBIL score due to prior defaults.
Mrs. Jaya Menon	₹3,09,450	700	Boutique Owner	₹35,870	Rented apartment; husband unemployed for 3 months; unstable income.
Mr. Jacob Mathew	₹2,12,500	755	IT Professional	₹60,450	Owns a house; vehicle loan EMI ₹11,460; debt-to-income ratio is healthy.

Problem Statement

The challenge is the assessment of creditworthiness of each applicant with the help of CIBIL scores, financial stability & various other risks. In the case of rejected applications, the bank must suggest to the applicant, what can be done to make the applicant eligible for future credit?

Detailed Analysis

1) Mr. Cheteshwara Pujara

a)   Assessment:

CIBIL Score: 830 (Excellent).
Income Stability: Monthly salary of ₹62,400 as a government servant.
Account Status: Savings account with VCB shows consistent and disciplined transactions.

b)   **Decision: Sanction the loan.**

Reasoning: His CIBIL score reflects strong creditworthiness, & his government job provides a stable income. He is a low-risk borrower.
Additional Insights:
Borrowers whose CIBIL scores go beyond 800 can negotiate for lower interest rates. Given his strong profile, Mr. Pujara may be offered preferential terms.

2) Mr. Reddy Gopal

a)   Assessment:

CIBIL Score: -1 (No credit history).
Income Stability: Regular farm income of ₹48,750/month with evidence of steady deposits in his VCB account.
Account Status: Consistent transactions indicate financial discipline.

b)   **Decision: Sanction the loan with conditions.**

Reasoning: Mr. Reddy has no credit score or less credit history, Farmers usually fall into that category. His regular income & disciplined banking habits mitigate this risk.
Conditions: Require a co-applicant or collateral to safeguard the loan.

c) **Recommendation for the Future**: Mr. Reddy should consider taking a small credit product, such as a credit card or an agricultural loan, to build a credit history.

3) Mr. Faiz Ahmed

a) **Assessment**:

CIBIL Score: 580 (Poor).
Income Stability: Monthly salary of ₹40,320 as a government employee.
Account Status: Having a salary account with VCB, however, his CIBIL score is low, suggesting he has defaulted in the past.

b) **Decision: Reject the loan.**

Reasoning: Having a CIBIL score of 300 to 600 means high-risk credit. Approving a loan at this score could damage the asset quality of banks.

c) **Recommendation for Future**:

Steps to Improve CIBIL Score:

- Clear outstanding dues promptly.
- Avoid applying for multiple loans simultaneously.
- Use a secured credit card to rebuild credit history.

Reapply for Loan: Once his CIBIL score improves to at least 650 & his repayment track record stabilizes.

4) Mrs. Jaya Menon

a) **Assessment**:

CIBIL Score: 700 (Intermediate).
Income Stability: Monthly income of ₹35,870 from a boutique.
Account Status: Her financial discipline is moderate but the husband is unemployed, and lives in a rental accommodation. This indicates financial vulnerability.

b) **Decision: Reject the loan.**

Reasoning: Even though she has an acceptable CIBIL score, her unstable financial condition and lack of any source of alternate income makes her at high risk.

c) **Recommendation for Future:**

Steps for Improvement:

- Diversifying income sources can strengthen financial stability.
- Ensure consistent growth in her boutique's income.
- Think about a joint application once her husband secures a stable job.

Reapply for Loan: Once her finances get stronger & other sources of income become evident.

5) Mr. Jacob Mathew

a) **Assessment:**

CIBIL Score: 755 (Good).
Income Stability: Monthly salary of ₹60,450 in the IT sector.
Account Status: Owns a house & has a vehicle loan with an EMI of ₹11,460. Debt-to-income ratio is well within limits.

b) **Decision: Sanction the loan.**

Reasoning: Mr. Mathew shows strong repayment capacity with a CIBIL score of above 750 & a healthy Debt-to-Income ratio.

Additional Insights:

IT sector borrowers generally have fixed income which makes them an attractive candidate for prospective loan schemes. With his current profile, Mr. Mathew could even explore refinancing his existing loan at a lower interest rate.

Key Learnings for Bankers

1) **Holistic Assessment is Critical:** Even though CIBIL score is an important indicator, it is not the only indicator to give you an accurate picture of a borrower's creditworthiness. The overall financial position of a borrower, the stability of income, and the banking habits also play an important role.

2) **Tailored Solutions for Applicants with No Credit History:** Borrowers like Mr. Reddy may lack formal credit records but exhibit strong financial discipline. With the help of a co-applicant or some guarantee, banks can sanction credit facilities.

3) **Proactive Credit Counseling**: Helping applicants with low/poor scores with ways to improve their creditworthiness will create a long-lasting customer relationship. It will also improve the financial literacy of the consumers contributing to overall economic growth.

Conclusion

This case study underscores the importance of a balanced & methodical approach to credit appraisal. The Vijayawada City Bank's wise decisions not only help the bank to safeguard its assets but also build a strong customer relationship by giving useful feedback to clients getting funded. As a banker, the ultimate goal is to enable financial inclusion while ensuring the stability of the institution.

* * *

CASE STUDY 7

BAILEE'S RIGHTS VS. OWNER'S CLAIMS: ANALYZING THE BANK'S STAND IN A CUSTODY DISPUTE

The Scenario

Sardar Manpreet Singh, a long-time customer of a branch, lost a packet containing five precious stones in the bank. Later on, a vigilant employee of the bank noticed the packet in the banking hall and handed it over to the Branch Manager. In the discharge of its fiduciary responsibilities, the branch put the pack in safe custody and made efforts to trace the rightful owner incurring substantial expenses.

A year later, Sardar Manpreet Singh came to the branch and claimed the packet. However, the Branch Manager refused to hand over the packet unless the claimant agreed to pay back the bank, the Safe Custody Charges and the expenses incurred in tracing the real owner. This raises a significant question: **Is the bank justified in withholding the packet?**

Legal and Practical Framework: The Finder of Lost Goods

The case is based on the principles relating to lost goods as well as the obligations of the finder under the Indian Contract Act, 1872. Below is a detailed examination of the applicable provisions:

1) The Finder as a Bailee:

    a) **Obligations of a Bailee (Section 151):** Under this section, the finder of lost goods is legally considered a bailee and is mandated to take care of the goods as a reasonable and prudent man. The bank's placing precious gems in safe custody and making proper enquiry for the owner thoroughly discharged its duty as a bailee.

    b) **Compensation for Services (Section 158):** A bailee may recover all reasonably incurred expenses for preserving the goods themselves or delivering them to the rightful owner. This section supports the bank's claim for reimbursement.

2) Rights of the Finder:

a) **Right to Retain Possession (Section 168):** This section empowers the finder to retain the goods until appropriate compensation for incurred expenses is paid. The bank is entitled to charge Safe Custody Fees and search costs in accordance with this condition.

b) **Right to Sell Goods (Section 169):** If the rightful owner does not pay the finder for his lawful expenses, the finder may sell the goods under certain conditions. However, this extreme measure must be justified by the value of the goods and the nature of the denial.

c) **Moral Obligation of the Finder:** Even with this right to possession, the finder, especially a financial institution, must ensure a proper balance between fiduciary duty with customer service and ethics. In this case, the bank behaved in a responsible manner by protecting valuable property and trying to find the owner.

Ethical and Operational Implications for Banks

1) **Financial Accountability:** As authorized by law, the finder can recover expenses, but since banks are professionals, they must keep records of what they did and how much it cost. This allows transparency and facilitates resolution in disputes of this type.

2) **Communicating Legal Provisions:** The bank should proactively communicate its position to the claimant and the legal grounds of its demand under Sections 158, 168 and 169 of the Indian Contract Act. Transparency helps alleviate customer dissatisfaction and reinforces the bank's reputation for fairness.

3) **Risk of Adverse Claims:** If the goods are not returned quickly after the settlement of a valid claim, the bank can be accused of negligence or mismanagement. The risks can be reduced by taking a structured approach within the ambit of law and good resolution to the customer.

Key Lessons for Bankers

1) **Legal Knowledge and Documentation:** Thorough understanding of the Indian Contract Act and proper documentation of efforts are critical in disputes involving lost goods.

2) **Balancing Legal Rights and Customer Service**: While protecting the interest of the bank, customer communication must be honest and courteous.

3) **Preservation and Reimbursement**: Banks should have clear mechanisms for addressing lost items, including the detailed cost accounting of lost items and information on reimbursement.

Conclusion: Was the Bank's Stand Justified?

The local Branch Manager's decision not to release the packet unless reimbursement is provided is legal. Sections 168 and 169 of the Indian Contract Act, 1872 provide a clear legal basis for the bank's demand for Safe Custody Charges and/or other reasonable expenses. Although the bank is entitled to act, it must act fairly and lawfully in the circumstances. The bank must communicate its position to the claimant in a way that conveys a fair and lawful intention.

* * *

CASE STUDY 8

RIGHT OF SET-OFF UNVEILED: CAN THE BANK RECOVER AN UNPAID OVERDRAFT FROM MULTIPLE ACCOUNTS?

The Scenario

A branch manager has to recover an overdraft of ₹15,000 allowed in the current account of Mr. Subhendu Chatterjee. Mr. Chatterjee has not paid up the outstanding amount despite repeated reminders. The branch has various accounts linked directly and indirectly with Mr. Chatterjee as under:

1) **Savings Account**: A joint account held by Mr. Subhendu Chatterjee and Mrs. Rina Chatterjee with a credit balance of ₹18,000.
2) **Current Account**: Operated in the name of M/s Chatterjee Electronics, a sole proprietorship owned by Mr. Subhendu Chatterjee, with a balance of ₹34,725.
3) **Recurring Deposit Account**: Held in the name of Miss Debarati Chatterjee, under the guardianship of Mr. Subhendu Chatterjee, with a credit balance of ₹7,000.
4) **Fixed Deposit**: A term deposit of ₹32,000 held by M/s Das and Chatterjee, a partnership firm where Mr. Subhendu Chatterjee is a partner.

The manager should find out whether the statutory right of set-off granted to the bankers will apply to these accounts so that the unpaid overdraft amount can be recovered.

Legal Framework

The **right of set-off** is a key tool available to banks, governed by legal principles and banking regulations in India. Under this right, a bank may adjust credit balances in one account to offset debit balances in another account held by the same customer. However, this right is subject to strict conditions, including:

1) **Same Name and Capacity**: The accounts must be in the same name and held in the same legal capacity. For instance, a personal account cannot be set off against a joint account or an account held in a fiduciary capacity.

2) **Legal Restrictions**: Most often than not, certain accounts like a minor account or a partnership account are legally protected and cannot be set-off against personal liabilities.

3) **Notice to the Account Holder**: While the bank may exercise this right, it is prudent and often legally required to notify the customer before doing so.

This right ensures that the banks are able to lessen the risk involved due to unpaid loans while also complying with the law.

Application of the Right of Set-Off

1) Savings Account (₹18,000):

This joint account, held by Mr. Subhendu Chatterjee and Mrs. Rina Chatterjee, has a credit balance of ₹18,000. Since the overdraft liability belongs to Mr. Subhendu Chatterjee alone, the joint account cannot be used for recovery. The rule of "same name and capacity" is violated here, as the account is jointly owned. Without explicit written consent from Mrs. Rina Chatterjee, the bank cannot exercise the right of set-off on this account.

2) Current Account (₹34,725):

Operated under the name of M/s Chatterjee Electronics, a sole proprietorship of Mr. Subhendu Chatterjee, this account qualifies for the right of set-off. A sole proprietorship is legally indistinguishable from its owner, and the credit balance can be applied to recover the overdraft in Mr. Chatterjee's personal current account. Since the sole proprietor and the individual are the same legal entity, this adjustment is both legally valid and prudent.

3) Recurring Deposit Account (₹7,000):

This account in the name of a minor, Miss Debarati Chatterjee, under the guardianship of Mr. Subhendu Chatterjee is law-protected. As per the banking regulation, a minor's account cannot be used to pay off the liability of the guardian. This account is held in a fiduciary capacity and as such is not subject to the right of set-off. Trying to adjust this account would both violate banking laws, and also attract legal consequences.

4) Fixed Deposit (₹32,000):

This term deposit is held by M/s Das and Chatterjee, a partnership firm in which Mr. Subhendu Chatterjee is a partner. Partnership assets are generally treated as separate from the personal assets of individual partners. Unless explicitly agreed upon in the partnership deed, the bank cannot use the firm's deposit to settle the personal liabilities of one of its partners. Therefore, this account is also ineligible for set-off.

Key Lessons for Bankers

1) **Evaluate Account Ownership and Capacity**: Before exercising the right of set-off, you have to see that the accounts have the same name and legal capacity to avoid disputes or legal challenges.
2) **Adhere to Legal Safeguards**: Protect the rights of joint account holders, minors, and partnerships, ensuring compliance with legal and regulatory requirements.
3) **Communicate with Customers**: Banks should always inform their customers why they are exercising their right of set-off in order to bring transparency and trust.

Conclusion

A review of the accounts indicates that the only current account of M/s Chatterjee Electronics having a balance of ₹34,725, is eligible for right of set-off. The bank in all safety may adjust the overdraft of ₹15,000 from this account. Thus, ₹19,725 will be left over in the account. The other accounts such as savings, recurring deposit or fixed deposit, cannot be used for recovery due to ownership structure, legal restrictions, or fiduciary obligations.

This case throws light on having a detailed understanding of the legal and operational aspects of the right of set-off so that the actions of the bank are compliant and that it can manage the risks efficiently.

* * *

CASE STUDY 9

UNLOCKING THE DEAD: NAVIGATING LEGAL COMPLEXITIES IN LOCKER ACCESS AFTER DEATH

When a Bank Locker Holder dies, the process to access his/her locker has to through strict legal and procedural norms to ensure fairness. Let us explore a scenario where a locker holder, Mr. K. Narayanan Nair, a resident of Kerala, has passed away in an accident. Mrs. Leela Narayanan, his wife, walks into the bank with the locker key and requests access to her deceased husband's locker to take anything valuable. Here is an elaborate way of how a professional banker must deal with this situation legally and lawfully.

The Scenario

Mrs. Leela Narayanan, while grieving the death of her husband, comes to the bank with a locker key and requests to access the locker. This request might seem simple but has legal and procedural complications that must be addressed to avoid unauthorized access and disputes amongst claimants.

Step-by-Step Process

1) Immediate Precautions Upon Notification of Death:

Upon receiving information about Mr. K. Narayanan Nair's demise, the following measures must be implemented promptly:

a)   **Marking Caution on the Locker Account:**

A sticker marked "Caution" is affixed to the locker, alerting staff to prevent any unauthorized operation. Also, the locker account in the bank system is marked *"Deceased- No access allowed"*.

b)   **Review of Locker Records:**

The locker-opening record is checked to see if any nominee was appointed by the deceased and that person is then contacted.

2) Verification of Nomination:

The handling of locker access heavily depends on whether Mr. Nair had nominated someone when opening the locker account.

If Nomination is Registered:

a) The bank identifies the nominee from its records. Let's assume Mr. Nair nominated his son, Mr. Ramesh Narayanan.

b) The process is as follows:

- The nominee is contacted and informed about his/her role in the locker operation.
- Mr. Ramesh is required to produce valid proof of identification and proof of relationship with the deceased.
- Access to the locker is arranged in the presence of two independent witnesses (e.g., senior bank staff or reputable individuals from the community).
- A detailed inventory of the locker's contents is prepared, listing every item. The inventory is signed by the nominee and witnesses to ensure accuracy and transparency.
- The nominee is allowed to take possession of the valuables, as listed in the inventory.

If Nomination is Not Registered:

In cases where no nominee exists, the approach depends on whether Mr. Nair left a will or not.

3) Access When a Will Exists:

If Mrs. Leela Narayanan produces a will left behind by her husband, then the bank requires her to produce a probate, which is a legal certification of the will by a competent court.

The process involves:

- Verifying the probate and that it covers the locker contents.
- Opening the locker in the presence of two independent witnesses, preferably senior bank officials or reputable individuals from the community or family.

- Preparing an inventory of the locker's contents under the supervision of bank personnel.
- Handing over the items to the executor or beneficiaries named in the will, as directed by the probate.

4) Access When No Will Exists:

The matter gets complicated when there is neither a nomination nor a will. The following steps are undertaken:

a) Mrs. Leela Narayanan must bring all legal heirs (e.g., children or other family members entitled to Mr. Nair's locker contents).

b) A Letter of Administration from competent court must be obtained. A letter of administration enables one or more of the legal heirs to administer the estate of a deceased.

c) The heirs file a joint claim letter with the bank confirming their consent to the locker operation and distribution of the locker contents.

d) The locker is accessed in the presence of the authorized heirs and two witnesses. As in previous scenarios, an inventory is prepared and signed by all parties.

e) The contents are distributed according to the consensus of the heirs or as instructed in the Letter of Administration.

Key Regulatory Guidelines

a) Indian Succession Act, 1925

This law governs how assets are passed on after one's demise. Under this law, nominees, executors or legal heirs are recognized, and in certain cases, a probate or Letter of Administration document is also required to distribute the assets.

b) RBI Guidelines on Locker Operations

The Reserve Bank of India (RBI) states, banks must act carefully and follow due process in allowing access to lockers of deceased persons. Some key provisions include:

- Locker access should only be given to the nominee or rightful legal heirs.
- An inventory must be prepared in the presence of witnesses.

- Banks must avoid unnecessary delays and provide guidance to claimants on the required documentation.

c) Banking Regulation Act, 1949

The act requires banks to be procedure-driven in dealing with the accounts and lockers of deceased customers. It requires locker operations to be transparent and accountable to avert any conflict or mismanagement.

Real-World Challenges and Practical Solutions

Challenge: Disputes Among Heirs

Multiple heirs often end up fighting over the division of the contents of the locker. For example, if Mr. Nair's kids do not agree on how to divide the contents, the bank must refrain from getting involved in resolving the dispute. The heirs should sort out the matter legally and must provide a court order or mutual agreement to the bank.

Challenge: Unavailability of Documents

If the claimants don't submit the required documents, for instance, probate or Letter of Administration the bank will not allow access to the locker. Instead, the bank should advise the claimants about the legal procedures to get the necessary documentation.

Key Lessons for Bankers

1) **Adherence to Legal Frameworks**

   Always comply with relevant laws and RBI guidelines to ensure fair and lawful handling of deceased customers' lockers.

2) **Empathy and Sensitivity**

   When dealing with grieving families, one must use compassion and clarity. Calmly explain procedures and assist them with the documentation needed.

3) **Detailed Documentation**

   Keep records of all the steps taken throughout along with copies of filed documents, inventories and signatures of witnesses. This protects the bank from potential legal challenges.

Conclusion

Dealing with the locker of a deceased customer, like Mr. K. Narayanan Nair, involves a fine balancing act of procedural diligence, legal compliance, and empathetic communication. By adhering to the rules and being open, bankers can prevent any complications or disagreements, keeping everyone safe and secure at all times.

* * *

ENDORSE AT YOUR OWN RISK: THE LEGAL FALLOUT OF A MINOR'S DISHONORED CHEQUE

The Scenario

There was a unique legal issue, when a minor Arjun issued a cheque in favour of Bidisha. Bidisha subsequently endorsed the cheque to Chiranjib, who passed it to Debashish, and ultimately, Debashish endorsed it to Eshita. Eshita, the Holder in Due Course (HDC), deposited the cheque in her bank account. But the cheque bounced back with the reason: "Insufficient Balance in Account".

After the instrument was dishonoured, Eshita gave a notice to Debashish demanding payment as she was the holder in due course. However, Debashish refused to comply, arguing that the ultimate liability rested with the drawer, Arjun, who, being a minor, lacked the capacity to contract and thus could not be held liable. This argument gave rise to several issues with regard to who was liable and the legal liability of the parties involved as per the Negotiable Instruments Act 1881.

Sequence of Events

Below is a sequence diagram illustrating the flow of endorsements:

1) **Arjun** (Drawer) → Issues cheque to → **Bidisha** (Payee)
2) **Bidisha** → Endorses to → **Chiranjib**
3) **Chiranjib** → Endorses to → **Debashish**
4) **Debashish** → Endorses to → **Eshita** (Holder in Due Course)

Legal Analysis

1) **The Minor's Role in Negotiable Instruments**

According to Section 26 of the Negotiable Instruments Act, 1881, a minor can draw, endorse or deliver a negotiable instrument. However, they cannot be personally held liable for the same as per the Indian Contract Act, 1872, as they lack contractual capacity.

In this case, Arjun is a drawer of the cheque who draws a cheque however being a minor he shall not be liable under the Negotiable Instrument Act, 1881. This principle prevents the holder in due course or any other party from recovering funds directly from Arjun, even if the cheque is dishonored.

2) **Rights of the Holder in Due Course (Eshita)**

Eshita, as the Holder in Due Course (HDC), holds a protected position under Section 9 of the Negotiable Instruments Act. This section guarantees that the HDC receives the instrument clear of any defects in title of previous parties and the HDC can enforce payment against all parties liable on the instrument.

Eshita's rights include:

a) **Claiming Payment:** She can recover the cheque amount from any party prior to her, including endorsers Debashish, Chiranjib and Bidisha.

b) **Defenses Invalid Against HDC:** Defense like Arjun's minority status cannot defeat Eshita's claim under Section 58.

3) **Liability of Endorsers**

Each endorser in the chain assumes liability toward subsequent holders unless expressly disclaimed. **Section 35** of the Negotiable Instruments Act states that every endorser is liable to compensate the holder in due course if the cheque is dishonored.

a) **Debashish's Role:** As an endorser, Debashish cannot absolve himself of liability by citing Arjun's minority. He is legally obligated to make the payment to Eshita.

b) **Subsequent Recovery:** After paying off Eshita, Debashish can recover from earlier endorsers including Chiranjib and Bidisha. Arjun, being a minor, is not subject to contractual obligations and therefore cannot be liable.

4) **Payee's Responsibility (Bidisha)**

As Arjun is a minor, his liability is nullified, but the payee Bidisha will be liable. The cheque's first payee Bidisha will be liable to subsequent parties as per the Negotiable Instruments Act. This shift ensures that Eshita can trace the liability chain back to Bidisha, bypassing Arjun's exemption.

Practical Implications

This case shows us how critical negotiable instruments are for minors. Here's how similar disputes can be approached:

Bankers' Responsibilities:

a) **Diligence in Verification:** When handling cheques, banks must check the drawer's capacity to contract. Although a minor can issue a negotiable instrument, the banks must check their potential liability in dishonor scenarios.

b) **Educating Customers:** Financial literacy drives must make customers aware of the consequences of accepting or endorsing a cheque from a minor.

Legal Strategy for Eshita:

a) **Enforcing Rights as HDC:** Eshita must sue Debashish, the immediate endorser. If it does not work out, she can escalate it to the prior endorsers, up to Bidisha.

b) **Exemption of the Minor:** Eshita's legal strategy must account for the reality that minor Arjun cannot be forced to pay.

Legal Provisions Referenced

a) **Section 26 of the Negotiable Instruments Act, 1881:** Recognizes a minor's instrument as valid, but the minor is not liable.

b) **Section 35:** Establishes the liability of endorsers toward the holder in due course.

c) **Section 58:** Protects the rights of the holder in due course against defective titles or disputes.

Key Lessons for Bankers

a) **Understanding Liability Chains:** A minor can draw a negotiable instrument, but his liability will be void, and the liability will be taken up by the subsequent endorser or payee.

b) **Holder in Due Course Protection:** Both the bank and the endorser must recognize that the rights of the HDC are protected by law even in the case of a minor.

c) **Legal Compliance:** Knowledge of sections 26 and 35 of the Negotiable Instruments Act goes a long way in adjudicating disputes and protecting the interests of stakeholders.

Conclusion

Debashish's argument that the liability is only on the minor drawer, Arjun, is not defensible in law. Arjun cannot be held liable as he is a minor, however, Debashish being the endorser is liable to the holder in due course Eshita. Once he pays Eshita, Debashish can recover his money from prior endorsers, including Bidisha, the payee. This distribution of responsibility guarantees security for the holder in due course and ensures the efficacy of negotiable instruments.

* * *

Letters of Credit Unraveled: A Banker's Guide to Spotting and Solving Export Finance Challenges

Introduction

Aryan Steel Industries, a legacy steel manufacturer established in 1970, had carved a niche in the domestic market by producing high-quality steel billets, bars, & wire rods. Even though it had a great past, increased cost of raw materials, higher energy prices in 2024, & insufficient working capital put financial pressure on the company. To turn the fate of the business around, Mr. Rohan, a young, dynamic MBA graduate & the third-generation leader of the family business, shifted his focus to international business. His decision to embrace exports brought new opportunities & challenges, highlighting the importance of Letters of Credit (LC) as a secure payment mechanism in global trade.

The Scenario

In July 2024, Aryan Steel Industries received its first export order, from the European firm Euro Steel GmbH, for €52,473. As a safeguard measure, Mr. Rohan recommended the use of an LC(Letter of Credit) for payment security. However, this strategic decision exposed the company to complex procedural, regulatory, & operational challenges that demanded careful navigation.

Financing Arrangements

Aryan Steel sought pre-shipment and post-shipment financing from its bank, National Trust Bank. The financial projections for export turnover were as follows:

- Total turnover (2024): ₹29,670,000.
- Export sales: ₹11,868,000 (40% of the total turnover).

- Raw material consumption: ₹8,749,200 (40% of ₹21,873,000).
- Working capital rotation period: 2.4 months (68 days).

The bank calculated the limit for packing credit at ₹1,640,406 after taking into account the rotation period (i.e. 2.4 rotation per annum on the basis of 12/2.4 rotation per annum). This facility ensured uninterrupted production and timely dispatch.

Problem Statement

How can Aryan Steel resolve procedural and compliance-related roadblocks in their LC transactions while undertaking multi-party trade operations in a financially secured way?

Detailed Analysis

1) Understanding the Letter of Credit Mechanism

Aryan Steel's reliance on LC underscored the importance of complying with the Uniform Customs and Practice for Documentary Credits (UCP 600). Key aspects of the LC mechanism included:

a) **Exporter Protection**: Ensured payment upon compliance with LC terms.
b) **Documentary Independence**: Banks dealt strictly with documents, not goods.
c) **Financing Opportunities**: Enabled pre-shipment & post-shipment financing.

The LC for €52,473 required shipment in 90 days & compliance was checked against the detailed documentary requirements.

2) Discrepancies in First Export Bill

After submitting the first export bill, the following discrepancies were noticed by Aryan Steel:

a) **Shipment Date Issue**: The Bill of Lading (dated August 16) exceeded the LC's latest shipment date of August 15. This contravened Article 29(b) of UCP 600, which extends expiry dates for non-working days but not shipment deadlines.

b) **Insurance Policy Mismatch:** The policy, dated August 20, was issued after shipment. As per article 28(e) of UCP 600 the insurance policy should match or precede the date of shipment.

c) **Partial Shipments:** The LC prohibited partial shipments, but multiple Bills of Lading evidenced different shipment dates. Although Article 31 of UCP 600 allows for more than one transport document for the same shipment, the terms of the LC being strict have made the presentation non-compliant.

d) **Currency Issue:** The LC was denominated in EUR, but the insurance policy was in INR. Article 28(f)(i) of UCP 600 requires alignment in currency for insurance coverage.

Result: The first export bill was thus rejected. This caused financial delay & reputational risk for Aryan Steel.

3) Second Export Order and Its Challenges

The second export order with Grande Metalworks Ltd. for €79,328 presented further challenges. Aryan Steel submitted two sets of Bills of Lading for the shipment, dated July 14 & July 15, covering 50 steel bars each. However, the LC strictly prohibited partial shipments.

Analysis: Article 31 of UCP 600 supports multiple transport documents for the same shipment if they align with a single journey. The shipments satisfy these criterion, thus the documents are technically compliant.

Outcome: The second bill was eventually accepted after rigorous scrutiny & communication with the advising bank.

4) Third Export Order and Bank Strike Issue

The third order for a sum of €63,194 faced an unusual event of a continuous bank strike from August 5 to August 13. The LC expired on August 10. As a result, Aryan Steel could not present documents within the validity period:

UCP 600 Perspective: Under Article 36, banks are not liable for interruptions by strikes or other force majeure occurrences. However, it does not extend credit validity during such periods.

Result: The third bill of export was declared invalid, costing financial strain & business loss.

5) Diversification into Modular Kitchens

To diversify revenue streams, Aryan Steel planned to trade modular kitchen sets in the US market. The firm received two orders from Steel Concepts Inc. of $125,472 but faced liquidity constraints.

Proposed Solution: Mr. Rohan chose a transferable letter of credit to trade without paying capital upfront.

Mechanism:

a) Steel Concepts Inc. issued a transferable LC for $125,472 through Global Bank USA.

b) Aryan Steel (First Beneficiary), made a payment of $94,104 to Star Modular Ltd. (Second Beneficiary), for procurement of kitchen sets costing $1,503 per set.

c) After the shipment, Aryan Steel presented its own invoice for $125,472 which was given to the issuing bank after keeping a profit of $31,368 (25%).

Key Clarifications for Transferable LC

1) Bank's Role in Transfers

The transferring bank retains discretion to accept or reject transfer requests, even if the LC is transferable. Article 38(a) of UCP 600 governs this discretion.

2) Permissible Changes in Transfers

As per Article 38(g) of UCP 600, changes that are permissible include:

a) Reduction in LC amount or unit price.
b) Curtailment of expiry/shipment dates.
c) Substitution of the First Beneficiary's name with the applicant's name.

3) Subsequent Transfers

Transferable LCs cannot be transferred beyond the Second Beneficiary, as per Article 38(d) of UCP 600.

4) Amendment Rejections

According to Article 38(f), when one party rejects an offer it will not invalidate the acceptance by other parties to the contract.

Key Lessons for Bankers

1) **Importance of Precision in Documentation**: Proper alignment with LC terms provides guarantee of smooth transactions & avoids expensive delays.

2) **Tailored Financial Solutions**: Banks must come up with tailor made financing products like transferable LCs for matching client specific needs.

3) **Proactive Risk Management**: If you can identify and address compliance risks early, it prevents financial or reputational risk.

Conclusion

Aryan Steel's journey highlights the critical role of LCs in facilitating international trade while exposing the complexities of compliance, documentation, & operational management. The firm was able to mitigate the challenges through strategic planning, following UCP 600 norms & by innovative use of transferable LCs.

* * *

Navigating RERA, SARFAESI, and IBC – How a Goa Real Estate Deal Turned into a Banking Nightmare

Introduction

Golden Sands Developers Ltd. (GSDL), a reputed real estate company based in Goa, launched an ambitious residential project in 2024. The project, comprising 42 premium flats, attracted significant attention, with each flat priced at ₹51.75 lakh. The flats were fully booked within the first 24 hours of the launch. But, due to a series of financial missteps & disputes involving GSDL, several banks, and homebuyers spiralled into a complex legal and regulatory mess. This case study explains the interplay of RERA, SARFAESI Act, & IBC and highlights the key challenges & learnings of various stakeholders in the banking & real estate sectors.

The Scenario

Golden Sands Developers Ltd. (GSDL) launched their project, "Coastal Haven," offering 42 premium flats in Panaji. Each flat was sold for ₹51.75 lakh and booking amount was ₹7.85 lakh collected from each allottee. Sale agreements were executed within 30 days of booking. On the launch day itself, a major local bank, Sunshine Co-operative Bank, established a counter offering aggressive home loans that covered 92% of the cost of the property. Many allottees took home loans from Sunshine Co-operative Bank by creating equitable mortgage on sale agreement and other documents. The bank also ensured proper registration of these mortgages with the Central Registry of Securitisation Asset Reconstruction and Security Interest of India (CERSAI).

In mid-2024, GSDL mortgaged the land on which "Coastal Haven" was being developed to Green Ocean Bank, securing a ₹19.6 crore working capital loan. This loan was raised without checking any prior encumbrances. Homebuyers claimed that this was a fraudulent act to obtain extra capital even after a mortgage was registered with CERSAI.

By the end of 2024, GSDL defaulted on its repayment obligations to Green Ocean Bank, which declared the loan a Non-Performing Asset (NPA). The SARFAESI Act was invoked by the bank to recover its dues through auction of project land. Worried by this development, many homebuyers approached the Goa Real Estate Regulatory Authority (Goa RERA) & the Debts Recovery Tribunal (DRT). Complaints were also filed with the Debts Recovery Appellate Tribunal (DRAT) and, subsequently, the National Company Law Tribunal (NCLT).

Problem Statement

Key concerns in this case include:

1) **Multiple Jurisdictional Challenges**: Figuring out the scope of RERA's jurisdiction with respect to SARFAESI and IBC in resolving disputes involving secured creditors & homebuyers.
2) **Rights and Interests of Homebuyers**: Ensuring the protection of homebuyers' investments & adherence to agreed terms under RERA.
3) **Resolution of Developer's Insolvency**: Balancing the interests of financial creditors, operational creditors, & homebuyers during insolvency proceedings.

Detailed Analysis

1) Loan Sanctions and Mortgage Registration

a) Sunshine Co-operative Bank offered loans worth ₹48.61 lakh per allottee (92% of the flat's cost). The loan process included equitable mortgages on sale agreements, KYC documents, & income proofs for the last three years.
b) To protect its interest, the bank got these loans registered with the CERSAI. Yet, before sanctioning the ₹19.6 crore working capital loan of GSDL, Green Ocean Bank did not check for existing encumbrances. This mistake shows how important due diligence is.

2) Conflict Between RERA, SARFAESI, and IBC

a) **RERA's Role**: Goa RERA, as per the Real Estate (Regulation and Development) Act, 2016, was approached by homebuyers alleging fraudulent financial practices by GSDL. The buyers demanded that the project land not be auctioned by Green Ocean Bank as it would impact their flats' delivery.

b) **SARFAESI's Enforcement**: Green Ocean Bank invoked SARFAESI provisions under Section 13(2), issuing a demand notice to GSDL for recovery of ₹20.32 crore (including interest and penalties). The bank proceeded with a property auction as per Section 13(4) but faced resistance from homebuyers who filed complaints with the DRT and DRAT.

c) **IBC's Precedence**: With mounting liabilities, GSDL filed for Corporate Insolvency Resolution Process (CIRP) under Section 10 of the IBC. The case was admitted by the NCLT who declared a moratorium under Section 14 which stayed all proceedings under RERA, DRT & DRAT, thus consolidating all claims under the insolvency process.

3) Rights of Homebuyers as Financial Creditors

a) According to the amended IBC (2018), homebuyers are recognized as financial creditors & can now participate in the Committee of Creditors (CoC). In this matter, homebuyers had a 45 per cent voting share in the CoC that enabled them to impact the insolvency resolution process greatly.

b) The CoC included Green Ocean Bank, Sunshine Co-operative Bank, & homebuyers. While the banks focused on recovering their debts, homebuyers merely wanted the project to be completed as promised.

4) Resolution Plan by Ocean Bay Construction Ltd. (OBC)

a) Ocean Bay Construction Ltd. (OBC) has submitted a resolution plan to the Green Ocean Bank for an amount of ₹21.5 crore to pay-off dues. The plan also included the completion of flats under revised architectural designs, with changes necessitated by structural reasons.

b) The plan required homebuyers to accept minor modifications while retaining the original price & specifications. Several home buyers objected citing RERA provisions of sticking to the original agreements.

Outcome and Rulings

1) **RERA's Position**: Goa RERA said it can deal with complaints against developers but it doesn't have jurisdiction over secured creditors such

as Green Ocean Bank. However, it instructed GSDL to ensure buyers' interests were safeguarded in the resolution process.

2) **NCLT's Decision:** The NCLT approved OBC's resolution plan, citing Section 31 of the IBC, which makes the plan binding on all stakeholders, including dissenting homebuyers. The plan's approval effectively nullified SARFAESI actions initiated by Green Ocean Bank.

3) **DRT and DRAT Proceedings:** Stayed under the moratorium declared by NCLT, consolidating all claims under the CIRP framework.

Key Learnings for Bankers

1) **Comprehensive Due Diligence:** Banks must do proper verification of existing charge through CERSAI to avoid conflict with other stakeholders.

2) **Understanding Legal Frameworks:** It is imperative to have knowledge of RERA, SARFAESI, IBC for tackling disputes involving overlapping jurisdictions

3) **Proactive Stakeholder Engagement:** Collaborating with homebuyers and other creditors can expedite resolution & minimize disputes.

Conclusion

The resolution plan proposed by Ocean Bay Construction Ltd. (OBC) was implemented successfully for completion of "Coastal Haven" and payment of dues owing to Green Ocean Bank. After early pushback, homebuyers were also fine with the amended terms and avoided more holdups.

* * *

Case Study 13

Banking on Ambition: When an Entrepreneur's Vision Meets a Credit Officer's Reality

Introduction

On a crisp morning in February 2024, the Jaipur branch of Rajputana National Bank (RCB) was flooded with loan applications from all across Rajasthan. Their recent Credit Camp proved to be a success. One important request was for a ₹15.47 lakh working capital loan from Aravalli Precision Tools (APT), a Jodhpur-based firm that was growing rapidly in the industrial machining business. Sunita Sharma, the senior credit officer, was known for her meticulous approach to credit evaluation. Although APT is financially sound and the company appears to have a lot of potential, Sunita's banking instincts tell her to be cautious with it.

Ramesh Rathore, APT's founder, was an ambitious entrepreneur seeking to scale his operations to meet the increasing demand. Sunita has a task at hand: **to make sure that the loan helps APT grow & also keeps the bank's financial interest safe.**

The Scenario

Ramesh Rathore, a 30-year-old entrepreneur from Ajmer, always foresaw making something bigger than life. A diploma holder in mechanical engineering, he worked as a machine operator at Tata Precision Industries for six years. Using his technical knowledge & entrepreneurial urge, Ramesh Rathore started 'Aravalli Precision Tools' in 2019. He took ₹4.28 lakh loan from a local cooperative bank. Starting small, the company operated out of a 1,050 sq. ft. rented space located in the industrial area in Jodhpur.

APT specialized in high-precision machining services, including milling, drilling, tapping, and turning, serving clients in the automotive, heavy machinery, & defense sectors. Equipped with machine tools of the highest precision coupled with a team of 10 skilled operators, APT becomes popular for quality & reliability.

By end of 2023, APT had orders worth ₹49.67 lakh for 2024. The company had got large orders from major clients like Marudhara Engineering (₹4.51 lakh), Infinity Systems (₹5.32 lakh) & Surya Engineering (₹3.97 lakh). To fulfill these orders, Ramesh applied for a ₹15.47 lakh working capital loan, which he planned to use for raw material procurement & labor hiring.

Problem Statement

Sunita faced several critical questions:

a) Will the ₹15.47 lakh loan be enough for APT to run and grow?

b) Was the collateral offered, primarily receivables and inventory, sufficient & liquid enough to mitigate risk?

c) Can the company handle the operational risks that come with growing fast without hurting its finances?

Her job was not just to approve or reject the loan. She needed to understand APT's financial & operational dynamics to make an informed decision.

Detailed Analysis

1) Business and Financial Overview

APT's financials revealed consistent growth over the years. The company's ability to offer high-precision machines service to demanding clients speaks volumes of its operational excellence.

Financials:

a) In 2022, net sales were ₹19.83 lakh, gross profit was ₹6.88 lakh, and net profit stood at ₹5.32 lakh.

b) In 2023, net sales increased to ₹37.92 lakh, with a gross profit of ₹10.36 lakh and a net profit of ₹6.21 lakh.

c) The 2024 (Projected) figures indicate net sales of ₹46.18 lakh, gross profit of ₹11.29 lakh, and net profit of ₹7.04 lakh.

d) The 2025 (Estimated) data forecasts net sales of ₹51.32 lakh, gross profit of ₹12.41 lakh, and net profit of ₹7.81 lakh.

APT's operational model includes:

a) Revenue Streams:

- – High-precision machining services.
- – Custom spare parts manufacturing for industries like automotive & defense.

b) Client Portfolio:

Over 60% of revenue came from three major clients: Marudhara Engineering, Infinity Systems, & Surya Engineering.

c) Operating Cycle:

- – Inventory turnover: 45 days.
- – Receivables turnover: 60 days.

While the numbers painted a promising picture, Sunita identified potential risks. APT has a cash conversion cycle of 60 days. Which is mainly dependent on receivables. Therefore, any delay in receivables means a liquidity issue for the company.

2) Loan Request and Collateral Assessment

Ramesh requested ₹15.47 lakh to meet the following expenses:

a) **Raw Materials Procurement**: ₹8.25 lakh for steel, aluminium, & other alloys.
b) **Labour Hiring**: ₹5.10 lakh for onboarding five additional operators.
c) **Miscellaneous Expenses**: ₹2.12 lakh for logistics & operational overheads.

Ramesh offered his receivables and inventory as a loan security:

A) Receivables: The receivables portfolio of APT stands at ₹16.21 lakh, with 78% of it concentrated among three major clients, posing a concentration risk.

a) Infinity Systems has the highest receivables at ₹5.32 lakh.
b) Marudhara Engineering follows with ₹4.51 lakh.
c) Surya Engineering accounts for ₹3.97 lakh.
d) The remaining ₹2.41 lakh is distributed among other clients.

B) Inventory: The inventory, which includes raw material, work in progress and finished goods was valued ₹8.95 lakh.

a)   Raw materials account for ₹2.34 lakh, representing the essential components for production.
b)   Semi-finished goods (work in progress) are valued at ₹3.65 lakh, indicating ongoing production.
c)   Finished goods, ready for sale, are worth ₹2.96 lakh.

Sunita was of the view that though the collateral coverage ratio was 1.63x, its liquid value would be insufficient under the stress scenario.

3) Advanced Credit Appraisal: Financial Projections and Risk Management

Sunita made up her mind to assess APT application through advanced techniques other than the usual MPBF formula. Her team thoroughly examined the financial projections of APT to determine the sustainability of the business in the long run and its capacity to repay the loan.

A) Financial Projections: APT's financial projections for 2024-2026 showed a steady growth path.

a)   2024 (Projected): Net sales of ₹46.18 lakh, gross profit of ₹11.29 lakh, & net profit of ₹7.04 lakh.
b)   2025 (Estimated): Net sales rising to ₹51.32 lakh, gross profit at ₹12.41 lakh, & net profit reaching ₹7.81 lakh.
c)   2026 (Estimated): Further growth with net sales at ₹56.45 lakh, gross profit increasing to ₹13.68 lakh, & net profit at ₹8.71 lakh.

Though the forecasts above seem rosy, Sunita noted the following:

a)   **Revenue Concentration:** More than 60% of expected revenues continued to be from the three main clients.
b)   **Working Capital Gap:** Raising the scale of operations would widen the working capital gap unless the management of receivables is improved.

B) Operating Cycle Analysis: APT's 60-day cash conversion cycle revealed the risk of liquidity gaps. Since nearly two months of receivables is tied up, the firm may have trouble conducting daily business.

C) Cash Flow Analysis: APT's cash inflow & cash outflow projection for 2024 showed a narrow buffer for contingencies.

a) **Projected Inflows:** ₹47.21 lakh (from sales).
b) **Projected Outflows:** ₹42.19 lakh (raw materials, labour, & overheads).
c) **Net Cash Surplus:** ₹5.02 lakh.

D) Stress Testing the Financials: Sunita's team did stress testing using various scenarios to check the robustness of the financial plan.

a) **Receivables Delays:** A delay of 30 days in the collection of receivables would result in increasing the cash conversion cycle to as much as 90 days, thus raising the working capital required by ₹ 5.38 lakh.
b) **Raw Material Price Volatility:** If raw materials cost increased by 10% then the gross profit margins would fall from 24.5% to 21.7% affecting liquidity.

E) Sectoral Risks: The machining industry in Rajasthan faced several risks:

a) **Supply Chain Volatility:** Relying on suppliers of raw materials like Marwar Steel & Ajmer Alloys made the industry vulnerable to price rises & delivery delays.
b) **Market Competition:** New players into the precision machining market could undercut APT prices affecting its market share.

4) Risk Mitigation Strategies

Based on her analysis of the situation, Sunita put forth the following measures to mitigate the bank's risk, while also help APT grow:

a) **Phased Loan Disbursement:** The funds should be released in tranches upon achieving operations milestones like procurement of raw material, accomplishment of certain orders, etc.
b) **Receivables Monitoring:** Mandate monthly reporting of receivables aging and collections to ensure timely inflows.
c) **Collateral Enhancement:** Ramesh should add other fixed assets like machinery to enhance security cover for the loan.
d) **Client Diversification:** Advise APT to expand its client base to reduce dependence on its top three clients.
e) **Credit Insurance:** Suggests credit insurance of the receivable against payment default.

5) Loan Structuring and Terms

Based on the findings, Sunita proposed a carefully structured loan with the following terms:

a) **Loan Amount** - ₹15.47 lakh
b) **Disbursement Schedule** - The loan will be disbursed in three tranches of ₹5.15 lakh each.
c) **Interest Rate** - The interest rate applicable is 10.5% (floating), subject to market fluctuations.
d) **Repayment Tenure** - The loan will be repaid over a period of 36 months.
e) **Moratorium Period** - A 6-month moratorium period is provided before the commencement of repayments.
f) **Collateral Coverage Ratio** - The loan is secured with a collateral coverage ratio of 1.5x.
g) **Additional Covenants** - The borrower is required to provide a monthly receivables aging report and undergo a quarterly inventory audit to ensure financial compliance.

The bank controlled disbursement, and APT would get operational support through this structure.

6) The Final Decision

After a comprehensive appraisal, Sunita and the credit committee approved the loan with the proposed terms. They stressed the importance of constant surveillance to make sure the covenants are being complied with.

Thanking the bank, Ramesh said the loan will help in business expansion. He promised to do the receivables management and also diversify his client base.

Key Lessons for Bankers

1) **Beyond Financials**: Credit appraisal must consider operational dynamics, industry risks, & borrower-specific challenges.
2) **Dynamic Loan Structuring**: The risks can be minimized with phased disbursement and customized covenants while also helping in the growth of business.
1) **Collaborative Approach**: When bankers tell borrowers about risk management strategies, it not only helps them to be sustainable but also strengthens the banker-client relationship.

* * *

CASE STUDY 14

FUNDING OR OVEREXTENDING? THE CRITICAL ROLE OF DRAWING POWER IN BUSINESS FINANCE

Introduction

Orange Agro Industries, a Nagpur-based agro-processing company, approached a consortium of banks in August 2024 to seek an enhanced working capital facility. With its business expanding rapidly in domestic and export markets, the company faced increased operational and financial demands. To meet these, the firm required a reassessment of its **Drawing Power (DP)** based on its latest financial data.

The consortium was tasked with arriving at the Drawing Power as per RBI approved norms under MPBF methodology as given in IBA Circular of September 2014. This exercise was extremely vital for ensuring the lending limits made in consonance with the actual operational needs of the company & also assessing margins and prudential norms.

The Scenario

Orange Agro Industries specializes in the processing and export of organic agricultural products. With growing orders from international buyers, the company needed increased funds to procure raw materials, store finished goods, and extend credit to its buyers.

The firm gave the consortium its financial information for the month of August 2024 which were:

Total Value of Stocks - ₹1,83,52,438
Sundry Creditors (Excess over assumed level) - ₹21,74,382
Eligible Trade Debtors - ₹61,45,786
Outstanding under Bills Discounted - ₹14,89,527
Stipulated Margin - 25%

Problem Statement

How should the Drawing Power for Orange Agro Industries be calculated, factoring in excess sundry creditors, net debtors, & the stipulated margin, to ensure the working capital facility is appropriately structured?

Detailed Analysis

To compute the Drawing Power of Orange Agro Industries, the bank's consortium applied MPBF methodology in a systematic way. Below is the detailed analysis:

Step 1: Net Value of Stocks (D)

The excess sundry creditors (over the assumed level) are deducted from the total value of stocks to arrive at the net stock value.

D = Total Value of Stocks − Excess Sundry Creditors
D = ₹1,83,52,438 − ₹21,74,382 = ₹1,61,78,056

Step 2: Net Value of Debtors (F)

The net value of trade debtors is calculated by deducting the outstanding bills discounted from the eligible trade debtors.

F = Eligible Trade Debtors − Outstanding Bills Discounted
F = ₹61,45,786 − ₹14,89,527 = ₹46,56,259

Step 3: Total Eligible Current Assets (G)

Total eligible current assets are determined by summing up the net value of stock (D) and the net value of debtors (F).

G = D + F
G = ₹1,61,78,056 + ₹46,56,259 = ₹2,08,34,315

Step 4: Stipulated Margin (H)

As per consortium norms the margin prescribed is 25%. This is applied to the total eligible current assets (G) to determine the margin.

H = Stipulated Margin × G
H = 25% × ₹2,08,34,315 = ₹52,08,579

Step 5: Drawing Power (DP)

Drawing Power is the total eligible current asset (G) less stipulated margin (H) of the borrower.

DP = G – H
DP = ₹2,08,34,315 – ₹52,08,579 = ₹1,56,25,736

Total Stock Value	A
Less: Excess Sundry Creditors (pertaining to Stocks) Excess of other sundry creditors beyond the level considered during the assessment.	B
Net Stock Value	D = A - B
Add: Eligible Trade Debtors, including advances for stocks and expenses as per assessment	E
Less: Outstanding Amount under Bills Discounted	BD
Net value of debtors	F = E – BD
Total Eligible Current Assets	G = D + F
Less: Margin as Stipulated	H
Drawing Power =	G – H

Final Calculation Summary

The Drawing Power for Orange Agro Industries is ₹ 1,56,25,736. The consortium decided this amount was the maximum that could be sanctioned for the working capital of the company considering the financial position.

Additional Context and Considerations

1) Consortium Lending Structure:

The banks consortium managing the working capital limits of Orange Agro Industries comprises of five banks with the shares as under:

a) Lead Bank: 40%
b) Member Bank 1: 20%
c) Member Bank 2: 15%
d) Member Bank 3: 15%
e) Member Bank 4: 10%

The sanctioned limits will be allocated among the consortium members in proportion to their Drawing Power.

2) Monitoring of Creditors and Debtors:

a) Sundry creditors exceeding the assumed level are often a red flag for delayed payments, which could indicate liquidity strain. Orange Agro Industries must ensure its payable cycle aligns with the assumptions made during the assessment.

b) The company must keep a close watch on receivables turnover to ensure prompt realisation of the trade debtors and not rely on bill discounting.

Key Lessons for Bankers

a) **Importance of Accurate Data:** A bank's ability to assess Drawing Power hinges on the accuracy and reliability of the borrower's financial data, including stock & debtor details.

b) **Adherence to Prudential Norms:** Compliance with RBI and IBA guidelines helps to ensure uniformity in the assessment of working capital requirements while protecting the bank's interest.

c) **Consortium Coordination:** In consortium lending, proper communication & proportional allocation of limits among member banks are vital for smooth operations & risk mitigation.

d) **Monitoring Margins:** The stipulated margin serves as a risk cushion for banks. Constant checking of margins ensures borrowers do not get over-leveraged.

Conclusion

Orange Agro Industries successfully demonstrated its financial standing through the submission of accurate stock and receivables data. Using the MPBF methodology, the consortium calculated the Drawing Power at ₹1,56,25,736, ensuring compliance with the RBI norms and mitigating the risk for the banks.

The case stresses the need for discipline in managing one's finances, especially one's stock, creditors, and debtors. The Drawing Power computed for Orange Agro Industries' is sufficiently comfortable for the company to operate as well as to remain financially prudent.

* * *

CASE STUDY 15

COLLATERAL OR CATASTROPHE? THE HIDDEN RISKS OF LOANS AGAINST LIFE INSURANCE

Introduction

Life insurance policies in India, issued by entities like the Life Insurance Corporation of India (LIC) & private insurers, serve dual purposes: providing financial security to policyholders & acting as collateral for loans. From endowment & term policies to fixed-term retirement policies, they cater to diverse customer needs, ensuring protection for dependents or old-age provisions. This case study looks at the acceptance of life insurance policies as security and uses a case study to highlight the difficulties as well as the opportunities for banks.

Scenario

Mr. Ramesh Verma, a 47-year-old small business owner from Pune, approached Southern India Bank for a ₹7.6 lakh loan to expand his printing business. Mr. Verma pledged an LIC endowment policy of ₹11,27,500 (sum assured) and ₹6,38,900 (surrender value) to secure the loan. The policy required an annual premium of ₹47,525 and had a term of 20 years.

The credit officer, Ms. Anjali Sharma, evaluated the proposal, considering the merits & risks of accepting the policy as collateral. Although it seemed appropriate, she had problems concerning its enforceability, premium continuity & underlying restrictive clauses.

Problem Statement

Should Southern India Bank accept Mr. Verma's life insurance policy as collateral for the proposed loan? What controls & measures must the bank put in place to mitigate risks relating to such advances?

Detailed Analysis

Merits of Life Insurance Policies as Security

a) **Legal Assignability:** Life insurance policies can be assigned under Section 38 of the Insurance Act, 1938. This ensures the bank's rights over the policy proceeds upon the borrower's default or death. In Mr. Verma's case, assigning the LIC policy gives Southern India Bank the first legal right to ₹11,27,500 (sum assured) or the accrued maturity benefits.

b) **Ease of Liquidation:** Compared to immovable property or stock, life insurance policies are highly liquid. If Mr. Verma defaults or dies, Southern India Bank can get back the loan amount through surrender value or sum assured of policy. This process involves minimal formalities, as evidenced by LIC's 98% claim settlement ratio in FY 2023-24.

c) **Minimal Supervision Needs:** Once assigned, the policy remains with the bank until maturity or settlement. Southern India Bank only needs to ensure timely premium payments, which can be automated through Mr. Verma's bank account.

Drawbacks of Life Insurance Policies

a) **Lapsation Risk:** If Mr. Verma does not pay the premium, the policy would lapse and its value to the bank would decrease. According to an LIC statistic, about 5.2% of policies lapsed in FY 2023-24 due to non-payment.

b) **Restrictive Clauses:** Policies may contain provisions like the "suicide clause," invalidating claims if the insured commits suicide within one year of the policy's commencement. Also, hazardous occupation clauses may void claims if Mr. Verma is involved in hazardous work.

c) **Limited Surrender Value:** Policies accrue significant surrender value only after completing 3–5 years. Mr. Verma's policy, which has a surrender value of ₹6,38,900, will not be sufficient to cover the loan of ₹7.6 lakh. Such a case would require a margin of 15%.

Precautions for the Banker

a) **Verify Insurable Interest:** The bank must confirm that insurable interest existed when the policy was issued. The insurable interest of Mr. Verma in his life was in terms of the provision of the Insurance Act, 1938.

b) **Check Proof of Age:** Southern India Bank must get LIC to verify Mr. Verma's age from an authentic document like a birth certificate or an Aadhaar card. Discrepancies may affect premium structure & claim settlement.

c) **Ascertain Surrender Value and Maintain Margins:** The bank has to check the surrender value from LIC records and keep a margin of 15%, which reduces the effective collateral value to ₹5,43,065. This ensures coverage for potential market or policy risks.

d) **Ensure Premium Continuity:** Automation of premium payment from the account of Mr. Verma reduces the risk of lapsation. Southern India Bank should allocate ₹47,525 annually to this account to cover the premium.

e) **Evaluate Policy Type:** Endowment policies are better than whole-life policies as they mature on a specified date or on the date of death of the insured. Thus, realization in the endowment policy is quicker. Mr. Verma's endowment policy aligns with this preference.

Resolution

Southern India Bank approved Mr. Verma's loan after a thorough risk assessment & implementing the following safeguards:

a) **Policy Assignment:** The policy was assigned to the bank under Section 38 of the Insurance Act, 1938, and the assignment was registered with LIC.

b) **Premium Automation:** Mr. Verma signed an agreement permitting his annual premium payments to be directly debited from his account.

c) **Margin Maintenance:** A 15% margin was maintained on the surrender value, reducing the effective collateral coverage to ₹5,43,065. The balance loan amount was secured through Mr. Verma's personal guarantee.

d) **Verification and Documentation:** Southern India Bank made sure that the LIC records confirmed the policy's validity, surrender value and proof of age.

Key Learnings for Bankers- Checklist: Advances Against Life Insurance Policies for Bankers

1) **Ensure Legal Assignment** – Ensure the life insurance policy has legal assignment in favour of the bank and it is properly registered with the insurance company.

2) **Verify Insurable Interest** – Verify that the Borrower had an insurable interest when the insurance policy was taken, and that the policy is valid and enforceable.

3) **Check Proof of Age** – Get the insurer to admit the age of the borrower officially, as premiums & policy validity depends on actual age.

4) **Assess Surrender Value** – Determine the surrender value of the policy before granting advances & maintain a margin of 5-10% on the surrender value for risk mitigation.

5) **Prefer Endowment Policies** – Give preference to endowment policies over whole life policies, as they mature earlier & provide better security for loans.

6) **Confirm Premium Payment Status** – Check that the policy is active & premiums are up to date; lapsed policies cannot serve as security.

7) **Identify Restrictive Clauses** – Be careful of specific clauses, like the "suicide clause" or hazardous occupations, which can affect the claim payout.

8) **Ensure Policy is Free from Encumbrances** – Verify that the policy is not pledged elsewhere or has any prior claims that could affect the bank's security interest.

9) **Keep Original Documents in Custody** – Get original policy documents duly stamped & signed, to ensure a valid claim in the event of default.

10) **Monitor Regular Premium Payments** – It must be advised to the borrowers to pay their premium regularly to prevent the lapse of the policy. It is difficult to revive a lapsed policy.

11) **Avoid Certain Policies as Security** – Do not accept children's endowment policies, deferred policies or policies under the Married Women's Property Act due to legal and liquidity issues.

12) **Handle Duplicate Policies Cautiously** – If there is an existing duplicate policy, check that the original has been lost and there isn't any fraudulent duplication in relation to the original. Otherwise, it may be misused.

* * *

CASE STUDY 16

DECODING STAMP DUTY: THE INTRICACIES OF MULTI-INSTRUMENT TRANSACTIONS IN BANKING

Introduction

In India, the levy of stamp duty is a fundamental requirement in validating documents that formalize property, mortgage, and financial transactions. The Indian Stamp Act 1899 Section 4 stipulates the stamp duty when more than one instrument is used in one single transaction. With the new amendments, especially the non-obstante clause that came into effect on July 1, 2021, the provisions have become increasingly complex in case of transactions in securities.

This case study dives into the nuances of stamp duty applicability with an exhaustive analysis of a real-world scenario, including legal precedents, financial figures, & implications for bankers. By breaking down the law's requirements & judicial interpretations, this study equips banking professionals with actionable insights for ensuring compliance & operational efficiency.

The Scenario: A Complex Property Transaction

Mr. Arjun Kumar, a Mumbai-based real estate developer, entered into a composite transaction to sell his commercial property aggregating worth ₹7,35,42,876 to a leading corporate. The transaction was structured as follows:

1) **Sale Deed:** A primary instrument transferring the ownership of the commercial property to the buyer, requiring a stamp duty payment of 5% of the sale consideration (₹36,77,143.80).

2) **Equitable Mortgage Declaration:** To finance the purchase, the buyer declared an equitable mortgage over the property to secure a loan of ₹5,00,15,647. The declaration, as part of the same transaction, was considered a secondary instrument under Section 4.

3) **Gift Deed and Financial Arrangement:** To meet his personal obligations, Mr. Kumar executed a gift deed transferring a part of the property (worth ₹1,25,00,000) in favour of his nephew along with a separate document for payment of monthly maintenance of ₹25,894.

4) **Maintenance Agreement:** A separate deed was executed between the corporate buyer & Mr. Kumar to provide for his upkeep post-sale, a condition for the buyer's acquisition of the property.

The complicated transaction made people question whether or how the stamp duty would be applicable on these multiple instruments.

Problem Statement

How should stamp duty be calculated when multiple instruments are used in a single transaction? Specifically:

a) Which instrument qualifies as the principal instrument?
b) What duties are chargeable on the secondary instruments under Section 4 of the Indian Stamp Act?
c) What is the impact of the 2021 amendment on the securities transactions?

Detailed Analysis

1) Legal Provisions under Section 4

As per Section 4 of the Indian Stamp Act, 1899:

a) **Principal Instrument:** The instrument which completes the transaction is liable to the stamp duty as prescribed.
b) **Secondary Instruments:** All other instruments related to the same transaction are chargeable with a nominal duty of ₹1 each.

But the 2021 amendment provided an exception in case of securities related transactions:

Non-Obstante Clause (Effective July 1, 2021): For the issue, sale, or transfer of securities, the instrument chargeable under Section 9A shall be treated as the principal instrument, & no additional duty is chargeable on other instruments.

2) Application to Mr. Kumar's Transaction

Each instrument was analyzed for its stamp duty liability:

Instrument	Role	Duty Liability
Sale Deed	Principal Instrument	₹36,77,143.80 (5% of ₹7,35,42,876)
Equitable Mortgage	Secondary Instrument	₹1 (Nominal duty under Section 4)
Gift Deed	Principal for Gift Portion	₹6,25,000 (5% of ₹1,25,00,000)
Financial Arrangement Deed	Secondary Instrument	₹1 (Nominal duty under Section 4)
Maintenance Agreement	Secondary Instrument	₹1 (Nominal duty under Section 4)

Total Stamp Duty: ₹43,02,146.80

3) Judicial Precedents

Numerous judicial pronouncements have explained the applicability of Section 4:

A) Case: Somaiya Organics Ltd. vs. Chief Controlling Revenue Authority (AIR 1972 All 252)

Scenario: Two declarations that supplemented sale deed, considered to be part of the same transaction.

Ruling: The sale deed was chargeable as the principal instrument, while the supplementary declarations attracted nominal duty.

B) Case: Maharaj Someshar Dutt vs. Krishna (ILR 7 Bom. 34)

Scenario: A gift deed and a related hypothecation agreement were deemed interdependent.

Ruling: Section 4 applied, with the gift deed as the principal instrument & the hypothecation agreement chargeable at ₹1.

C) Case: Someshwar Dutt vs. Revenue Authority

Scenario: Multiple instruments, including maintenance agreements & sale deeds, were examined.

Ruling: Only the principal instrument attracted full duty and the remaining were chargeable at ₹1 each.

4) Impact of the 2021 Amendment

The 2021 amendment simplified transactions involving securities:

a) **Prior Practice:** Every instrument in a securities transaction was independently assessed for duty.

b) **Post-Amendment:** Only the principal instrument under Section 9A is chargeable, significantly reducing compliance costs & complexity.

5) Key Considerations for Bankers

The bankers must keep the following in mind while dealing with multi-instrument transactions:

1) Identify the Principal Instrument:

a) Find the instrument that completes the transaction.

b) Wrong classification may lead to fines & compliance problems.

2) Leverage Nominal Duty Benefits:

Get the documentation done so you can enjoy the low duties on the secondary instruments.

3) Compliance with State-Specific Laws:

Stamp duty rates and regulations differ across states (e.g. if you transfer property in Maharashtra, the state charges around 6% of the value(varies from time to time). By contrast, this duty in Gujarat is only 4.9% of the property value).

4) Special Considerations for Securities:

All transactions related to securities have to comply with Section 9A as amended in 2021.

Key Learnings for Bankers

1) **Comprehensive Transaction Structuring:** The banker must ensure that the transactions are structured so as to reduce the stamp duty liability, while also maintaining compliance with laws.

2) **Regular Updates on Amendments:** Keeping up with changes such as the 2021 amendment will help in lowering compliance costs & increasing operational efficiency.

3) **Focus on Legal Precedents:** Knowing the court rulings helps us in solving problems and advising clients.

Conclusion

This case study illustrates the critical role of Section 4 of the Indian Stamp Act, 1899, in determining stamp duty liabilities in multi-instrument transactions. By identifying the principal instrument & leveraging statutory provisions, bankers can ensure cost-effective and legally compliant operations. In the wake of constantly changing stamp duties rules & regulations across states and the introduction of new amendments, the banking profession has to become more dynamic, requiring the skills of professionals like never before.

* * *

BALANCING REGULATIONS AND COMPASSION: RESOLVING CLAIMS FOR MISSING PERSONS IN BANKING

The Scenario

Mrs. Radhika Sharma, a resident of Lucknow, approached your branch with a harrowing story. Her husband, Mr. Ashish Sharma, went missing two years back, leaving her to navigate life's challenges alone. To ease her financial problems, she has sought to claim a fixed deposit of ₹1 lakh in her husband's name of which she is the nominee. As a Branch Manager of a reputed public sector bank, it is upon you to handle her claim case within the complex legal and procedural framework governing the same.

Legal and Regulatory Framework

According to Section 108 of the Indian Evidence Act, 1872, there is a rigorous standard for presumption of death in the case of missing persons. A person is presumed dead if he has not been heard of for seven years. Until such a declaration is secured from a competent court, the legal heir or nominee cannot settle claims like fixed deposit, insurance, or any other account.

Given the difficulties that were being faced, the RBI provided a major relaxation. According to the RBI's Master Circular on Customer Service in Banks, small-value claims of up to ₹1 lakh can be settled without a death certificate, under certain conditions. The aim of this guideline is to impose a balance between the regulatory burden and immediate funding needs of claimants.

Process for Settlement of Claims

For cases like Mrs. Sharma's, the bank must adhere to the following steps:

1) Documentary Evidence: The claimant must submit:

a) **First Information Report (FIR):** This is the first proof of Mr. Sharma being reported missing.

b) **Non-traceable certificate:** is a document issued by police which showcases Mr. Sharma could not be found despite attempts.

c) **Indemnity Bond:** A legal undertaking from Ms. Sharma indemnifying the bank against any future liabilities should Mr. Sharma reappear.

2) Threshold Limit Compliance: Claims worth ₹1 lakh or less can get settled without any death certificate. The branch has to confirm that this claim is within that limit and Mrs. Sharma has provided all documentation.

3) Authority Approval: The claim must be reviewed and approved by the **Assistant General Manager (Admin)** of the Administrative Office.

For claims over ₹1 lakh, a court declaration is required under Section 108, which presumes the death of the missing person. Banks must comply with this procedure carefully to avoid legal and reputational risks.

Critical Managerial Interventions

Being a seasoned Branch Manager, you have to make sure that Mrs. Sharma's case is handled sensitively while complying with procedure.

1) Navigating Legal Intricacies:

Start by explaining Mrs. Sharma the provisions of Section 108 and under what scenario claims of missing persons are made under the Act. Acknowledge her pain while setting reasonable expectations for the timeline and needs.

2) Facilitating Documentation:

Assist her in liaising with local authorities to procure the FIR and the non-traceable certificate. Provide templates or examples for indemnity bonds to simplify the process.

3) Expedited Resolution:

Once the documents are submitted, coordinate with the Administration office to take her case on priority. Use your contacts to get things done faster and to follow RBI norms.

4) Risk Mitigation:

Conduct thorough due diligence on the claim. Be vigilant about all documentation, especially the FIR and the police report to guard against frauds or disputes.

Key lessons for Bankers : Checklist for Handling Claims for Missing Persons

1) **Empathy Meets Compliance**: Bankers must handle missing person cases with care, ensuring that procedures do not add distress to the claimants. Sensitivity in communication is key, making the process smoother & less burdensome.

2) **Regulatory Precision**: Familiarity with Section 107/108 of the Indian Evidence Act, 1872, is necessary for the assessment of claims. By following RBI guidelines, claims are settled legally, effectively & efficiently.

3) **Essential Documentation**: FIR & a non-traceable police report are necessary. A letter of indemnity must be obtained. A court order is required after seven years.

4) **Threshold & Policy Adherence**: Banks should set threshold limits for claims to minimize documentation. A streamlined approach reduces delays while ensuring security.

5) **Proactive Advocacy & Support**: Banks must guide claimants through legal & bureaucratic steps, ensuring a smooth & customer-friendly experience.

* * *

CASE STUDY 18

THE ₹500 CHEQUE THAT BECAME ₹8,500: A CASE OF BANKING NEGLIGENCE OR SMART FRAUD?

The Scenario

Mr Rajiv Sharma, a longstanding customer of your Bank's Amritsar Branch, issued a cheque for ₹500 dated March 31, 2024. The cheque was presented on 05.04.2024, however; the Bank paid an amount of ₹8,500. A month later, Mr. Sharma saw this while updating his passbook and immediately told the bank about the discrepancy. The cheque that he issued was tampered with, and the bank was negligent according to him.

Subsequent forensic examination of the cheque under an ultraviolet ray lamp revealed that the name of the payee, the amount, and the date had been chemically altered. Mr. Sharma questioned the bank's diligence, alleging that it failed to detect the forgery before processing the payment. The matter called for a detailed legal and procedural review of the bank's liability.

Key Legal Provisions and Their Implications

1)Section 10: Payment in Due Course (Negotiable Instruments Act, 1881):

This section defines "payment in due course" as a payment made in accordance with the apparent tenor of the instrument, in good faith, and without negligence. For the bank to invoke this protection, the cheque must appear genuine to a reasonable person examining it in normal circumstances.

2)Section 89: Banker's Discharge for Materially Altered Instruments:

Section 89 provides that if a cheque is materially altered but the alteration is not apparent, the bank is discharged from liability if it pays in good faith as per the cheque's apparent tenor. The protection under this section is critical in cases where alterations are sophisticated enough to evade detection during routine scrutiny.

3)Section 131: Banker's Protection in Good Faith Collection:

Although primarily applicable to instruments collected for third parties, it indicates the general rule that banks will not be liable if the act has been done in good faith and without negligence.

4)Banking Standards and Operational Procedures:

a) Cheque Verification Mechanisms: The bank uses the visual and mechanical testing of cheques, which includes ultraviolet or watermark testing for cheques of large value. But small value cheques are not subject to any such process in the routine course.

b) Customer's Role: It is the duty of the customer to keep their instruments secure. Mr. Sharma's lack of diligence in protecting the cheque could be an argument put forth by the bank.

Deep Dive into Bank's Defense

Was the Bank Negligent?

For negligence to be established, Mr. Sharma must prove that the bank failed to exercise reasonable care expected in processing cheques. Here, the alteration was not apparent under normal scrutiny. Detection required ultraviolet examination—a process not standard for all cheques. The bank, therefore, acted in line with standard industry practices.

Did the Bank Act in Good Faith?

The payment was forged without knowledge or suspicion of forgery. The cheque was processed according to its obvious tenor and therefore constituted a payment in due course.

What Could the Bank Have Done Differently?

In this case, the bank is not legally liable. But if it had had some measures like compulsory UV checks for all cheques above a certain limit, then it could have prevented this. This incident also tells us the importance that customers should receive real-time alerts of cheques.

Final Verdict:

As the alterations were undetectable on normal scrutiny and payment was made in good faith, the bank will not be liable for the fraud due to the provisions of Sections 10 and 89 of the Negotiable Instruments Act, 1881. Nonetheless, this case shows how banking practices must change to counter cheque frauds that are being committed.

Key Lessons for Bankers

1) Proactive Fraud Detection Mechanisms:

    a) Use AI-based fraud detection systems to check for unusual cheque patterns.

    b) Increase the frequency of random UV lamp checks for cheques of any amount.

2) Customer Education on Cheque Handling:

    a) Arrange workshops or campaigns to secure the cheque book from an unauthorized alteration.

    b) A positive pay system needs to be introduced for hassle-free payment of cheques.

3) Strengthening Operational Protocols:

    a) Revise internal cheque-clearing checks, including forensic checks for significant (high-risk) payments.

    b) Use real-time alerts to customers for cheque clearing so that they can intervene immediately.

* * *

Case Study 19

The ₹25,000 Dilemma: A Banker's Guide to Navigating Court Attachments and Compliance

The Scenario

Dealing with court attachment orders is a complex affair and requires an adequate idea of the law and banking. The case study represents Mr. Sinha who has several accounts, transactions and an attachment order of ₹25,000. The handling of each transaction will depend on the legal characterization of the transaction which is a debt "owing or accruing due." The treatment of each transaction is discussed in detail below.

Legal Framework

Court attachment orders are defined under Section 60 of Code of Civil Procedure (CPC), 1908. Such an Order will attach debt which is "owing and accruing" to the judgment-debtor at the time of receipt of the Order. The words "owing" mean payable now and "accruing due" means amount due in the future sometime but not yet realized. This difference is important in deciding what assets and transactions are covered by the order of attachment.

Analysis of the Transactions in the accounts of Mr. Sinha

1) Draft Purchase for ₹15,000

Action: Not attached.

Explanation: The funds tendered by Mr. Sinha for the draft do not constitute a debt "owing or accruing" as they are in transit to be converted into another instrument. At the time of the attachment order, these funds are not held by the bank as a payable liability to Mr. Sinha.

Regulatory Basis: Circulars from the Reserve Bank of India (RBI) clarify that attachment orders cannot seize funds that are in the process of being converted into other instruments unless explicitly directed.

2) Joint Account with Wife (₹5,000)

Action: Not attached.

Explanation: Joint accounts operate under a contractual agreement with all account holders, and their attachment requires explicit inclusion in the court order. Since the order is in Mr. Sinha's sole name, his proportional share in the joint account cannot be attached without further legal instruction.

Legal Note-In India, typically joint bank accounts are safe from attachment orders directed only against one account holder. The protection arises from the principle that the funds in a joint account are treated as co-owned; so, attaching the account for the one holder's debt is unfair to the other co-owners. So without specific orders or all the account holders included in the court order, the money in such joint accounts is not attachable.

3) Credit Voucher of ₹7,000 (Statutory Charges Realized)

Action: Attached.

Explanation: Once proceeds have been realized and credited, it becomes "owing" to Mr. Sinha. The key question is the time of realization, which took place before the receipt of the order of attachment. These funds are available and payable and fall within the scope of order.

Compliance Note: The amount must be frozen by the bank and reported to be available as per the court's order.

4) Draft for ₹7,500 Presented and Credited

Action: Attached.

Explanation: Similar to the statutory charges, once the draft amount is credited to Mr. Sinha's account, it becomes a debt "owing" to him. This amount is, therefore, subject to the attachment order.

Operational Challenge: The bank must be careful so that these proceeds aren't released by mistake, otherwise, the bank will be liable for penalties under the CPC.

5) Clearing Cheque for ₹2,000 Tendered by Mr. Sinha

Action: Not attached.

Explanation: The cheques given for clearing are expected future credits to be earned. These funds are not "owing" or "accruing" at the time of attachment and therefore are outside the order.

Key Insight: The bank must track the clearing process but cannot freeze or divert these funds unless the attachment order is amended to include future credits.

6) Overdrawn Current Account (-₹5,000)

Action: Not attached.

Explanation: An overdrawn account reflects a liability owed by Mr. Sinha to the bank, not the other way around. Attachment orders cannot be executed on amounts that do not constitute a net credit balance.

Practical Consideration: The bank must communicate the status to the court to avoid unnecessary follow-up.

Legal Implications and Compliance

The branch manager has to follow the procedural requirements provided under the CPC and the banking regulations:

a) **Freeze and Report:** Any funds that are deemed "owing or accruing" should be frozen at once, and a compliance report must be submitted to court in time.

b) **Segregate Transactions:** Make a clear distinction between realized and unrealized credits and between sole and joint accounts.

c) **Customer Communication:** Inform Mr Sinha about the attachment order and its implications without sharing confidential court instructions.

Key Lessons for Bankers

When dealing with court attachment orders, it is essential to evaluate the status of each transaction based on the following principles:

a) **Verify Order Authenticity:** Make sure the order of attachment is issued from competent authority viz, court, Income-tax department, Enforcement Directorate, etc. and is proper with seals and signatures.

b) **Identify the Type of Attachment:** Review whether the attachment is under the Code of Civil Procedure, 1908 (CPC), Income Tax Act, 1961, or other applicable laws. Different regulations govern salary, tax, and debt-related attachments.

c) **Match Account Holder Details:** To prevent erroneous action, verify and confirm the account holder's name, PAN, Aadhaar, account number and others mentioned in the attachment order.

d) **Assess Account Type:** Determine if the account is individual, joint, or term deposit (TD). As per Income Tax Act, joint accounts are presumed to have equal shares, and only the debtor's portion can be attached.(In India, typically joint bank accounts are safe from attachment orders directed only against one account holder.)

e) **Check for Exemptions:** Verify whether the attached funds qualify for exemptions under Section 60 of CPC (Salary Protection), Provident Fund Act, or other legal provisions. Certain deposits (PPF, pension) are not attachable.

f) **Freeze the Account or Transfer to Suspense Account:** If the attached amount is in Current/Savings (CA/SB) accounts, transfer it to a suspense account or block access. For Fixed Deposits (TDs), mark the system as "Under Attachment."

g) **Inform the Account Holder:** Notify the customer via Registered Post or electronic communication about the attachment, the amount frozen, and the procedure to seek a release order if applicable.

h) **No Foreclosure or Loan Against Attached Funds:** If a Fixed Deposit (FD) is attached, ensure that no premature withdrawal, foreclosure, or loan against it is sanctioned.

i) **Comply Within Timeframe:** Perform the act in a timely manner to comply with the law. Any delay or default may result in action against the bank.

j) **Maintain Proper Records:** Make sure to record every action taken, indicating which order it relates to, the date the action was performed, the interaction had with the account holder, and what the status is, as this will be referred to during audits and regulatory inspections.

* * *

CASE STUDY 20

NAVIGATING EXTRAORDINARY CHALLENGES: A BANKER'S ETHICAL AND LEGAL RESPONSE TO A MEDICAL EMERGENCY

The Scenario

Mr. Srinivasan is a retired government officer and a long-term customer of your branch. He is holding a Term Deposit Receipt (TDR) of ₹3,00,000 and a Savings Bank (SB) account that is operated in a satisfactory manner for collecting his pension. On one fine day, the branch is informed by his neighbour Mr. Ramesh that Mr. Srinivasan is unconscious due to a cardiac arrest and is in a nursing home. A sum of ₹20,000 has been spent on emergency treatment so far. Mr. Ramesh requests ₹10,000 to be paid to the nursing home for continued treatment.

This poses a challenge for the bank: how to act quickly enough to help a valued customer while complying with banking norms and protecting the bank's interest.

Deconstructing the Problem

1) **Verification of Circumstances:** Just because the demand is urgent doesn't remove the banks' obligation to check the facts. A senior officer of the bank should visit the nursing home instantly to ascertain Mr.Srinivasan's health status. This will ensure that the claim of Ramesh is genuine. During the visit, the officer can collect supporting evidence such as hospital bills and medical reports.

2) **Customer Consent and Legal Authority:** Since Mr. Srinivasan is unconscious and unable to provide the required authorization (signature or thumb impression) for withdrawal, this creates a procedural limitation. However, extraordinary circumstances like these call for an ethical and practical response, weighing procedural adherence against the urgent need for action.

Proposed Solution

After confirming the authenticity of the situation and ensuring that the immediate family is unavailable, the bank can proceed with the following measures-

1) Release of Funds with Safeguards: The amount of ₹10,000 can be debited from the Savings Bank account of Mr Srinivasan and paid directly to the nursing home subject to the following conditions.

a) Obtain a formal receipt from the nursing home acknowledging the amount and explicitly mentioning that it is for the treatment of Mr. Srinivasan.

b) Document Mr. Ramesh's role in conveying the situation and secure his signed statement as a record.

2) Witness Support: The signatures of two respectable neighbors present at the nursing home should be obtained as witnesses on the debit voucher. Their testimony ensures the decision is backed by credible external verification.

3) Exceptional Nature of the Decision: Given the significant quantum of deposits, and satisfactory conduct of the account of Mr. Srinivasan, this extraordinary action is a step justified as an act of trust and service. While it's not standard operating procedure, the bank does this to help out in times of emergency.

Legal Justification Under Quasi-Contract

The quasi-contract principle under section 69 of the Indian Contract Act, 1872, gives a strong backing to the bank's action. This section states:

"A person who is interested in the payment of money which another is bound by law to pay, and who therefore pays it, is entitled to be reimbursed by the other."

In this context:

1) **Beneficiary.** For whom the expense is incurred- Mr. Srinivasan.
2) **Third Party.** The bank- acting in good faith to meet an essential need.
3) **Reimbursement Obligation.** Mr. Srinivasan (or his legal heirs) shall be liable to repay a bank to ensure that the bank does not suffer any loss.

The principle invoked provides defence to the Bank's actions, even if there were to be a dispute which is unlikely.

Enhanced Risk Mitigation

To further protect the bank:

a)   Record the rationale and decision in the branch log, approved by the branch manager or a higher authority.
b)   Attempt to notify Mr. Srinivasan's family or legal heirs about the bank's action as soon as possible.
c)   Retain all relevant documents, including medical bills, debit vouchers, the nursing home's acknowledgment, and statements from witnesses, for compliance and audit purposes.

The Broader Perspective

Balancing banking rules with compassion and a sense of ethics is the need of the hour. Through its prompt actions, the bank helps Mr. Srinivasan get timely medical treatment while also enhancing the image of the bank as customer-friendly and socially responsible.

Key Takeaways for Bankers

a)   **Customer-Centric Decision-Making:** In extraordinary situations, bold steps are needed to ensure customers' interests are protected while safeguarding those of banks.
b)   **Legal Awareness:** Knowledge of principles like quasi-contracts helps bankers to act in unusual situations.
c)   **Comprehensive Documentation:** Proper documentation and supporting evidence can help you avoid disputes as well as prove compliance.

* * *

CASE STUDY 21

Fraud, Negligence, or Bad Banking? The Legal Fight Over a ₹1,73,500 Dishonored Cheque

The Scenario

The Odisha City Urban Bank (OCUB) bought a cheque for loan installment worth ₹1,73,500 from its customer, Shri Subrat Dash and presented it to the drawee bank for payment. The cheque was initially returned with the remark, "Endorsement requires bank's confirmation." OCUB subsequently confirmed the endorsement and re-presented the cheque for payment. The drawee bank returned the cheque again with the reason "refer to drawer". When OCUB approached Shri Subrat Dash for recovery of ₹1,73,500, he refused to pay the said amount contending that the first time the cheque was presented there were sufficient funds in the account and the bank returned the cheque due to the mistake of it. Mr. Subrat also argued that the bank should have informed him of the cheque's return after the first presentation. He further insisted that as the bank did not give him notice, it should bear the loss.

Legal and Procedural Analysis

1) Role of Odisha City Urban Bank as a Holder for Value

When OCUB bought the cheque from Shri Subrat Dash, OCUB became a holder for value with regard to the cheque by virtue of Section 8 of the Negotiable Instruments Act, 1881. In other words, OCUB was authorized to present the cheque for payment and entitled to receive payment from the drawee bank or the drawer in the event of dishonour.

When the bank became the holder for the value of the cheque, the bank not only became the owner of the cheque but also took the associated right to claim that amount when the payment is refused. It is important for the bank to protect itself financially and to be able to hold the drawer responsible in such situations.

2) Initial Return of the Cheque for Technical Reasons

The first return of the cheque with the remarks that "endorsement requires bank's confirmation" was a procedural issue and not an outright dishonour. This type of return typically occurs when there is a discrepancy or ambiguity in the endorsement chain, requiring additional verification. OCUB took the proper steps to fix the technical problem, confirming the endorsement and re-presented the cheque for payment.

Since the initial return did not constitute dishonor, OCUB was under no obligation to inform Shri Subrat Dash at this stage. Notification is generally mandated only in cases of dishonor, not for technical returns that do not reflect a refusal to pay.

3) Dishonor of the Cheque on Second Presentation

When the cheque was presented a second time, it was returned with the remark "refer to drawer." This is a clear case of dishonor. In the bankers' terminology, it means there are insufficient funds or there are other issues with the account that prevent payment.

As per Section 31 of the Negotiable Instruments Act, 1881, it is the drawer's duty to ensure adequate funds are available in the account to honor the cheque. Failure to do so makes the drawer liable for the dishonor. This responsibility is not mitigated by any procedural delays or technical issues during the initial presentation.

4) Drawer's Argument: Notification Obligation of OCUB

Shri Subrat Dash's claim that the bank should have notified him after the cheque was first returned is unfounded. The law mandates banks to inform the drawer only when a cheque is dishonored. Since the first return was a technical issue and not dishonor, there was no requirement for OCUB to notify Shri Subrat at that stage.

Moreover, upon the second presentation of the cheque, the OCUB sought a refund from Shri Subrat, thus, it has done its duty as holder for value. The bank acted under its rights and in accordance with banking practice.

5) Liability of Shri Subrat Dash

Shri Subrat Dash's refusal to refund ₹1,73,500 is not legally valid. According to Section 30 of the Negotiable Instruments Act, 1881 the drawer of a cheque shall compensate for a loss suffered by the holder (in this case OCUB) on the dishonour of the cheque, given the cheque was presented in the validity period and in proper form.

Shri Subrat's claim that the bank ought to suffer loss due to the first technical return by the bank cannot absolve him of liability. The cheque was eventually dishonoured on account of insufficient funds or other reasons for which his account was liable, making him responsible to refund the amount to the bank.

Legal Framework Supporting OCUB's Position

a) Negotiable Instruments Act, 1881:

- **Section 8:** Defines the holder for value and their rights.
- **Section 30:** Establishes the liability of the drawer for dishonored cheques.
- **Section 31:** Imposes a duty on the drawer to ensure sufficient funds are available to honor a cheque.

b) **Banking Standards and Codes Board of India (BSCBI):** Banking codes also emphasize the drawer's obligation to maintain sufficient funds and do not place the onus of technical returns on banks unless dishonor occurs.

Key Lessons for Bankers

a) **Role as Holder for Value:** Banks purchasing cheques must understand their rights and obligations as holders for value and act promptly to safeguard their financial interests.

b) **Customer Communication:** Banks need to maintain transparency with their customers but are responsible only to inform customers in case of dishonor and not technical faults.

c) **Legal Recourse:** In case of dishonour, banks must be in a position to exercise their legal rights under the Negotiable Instruments Act for quick recovery.

Conclusion

Odisha City Urban Bank acted in accordance with legal and procedural norms. As the holder for value, it has the right to recover the ₹1,73,500 from Shri Subrat Dash. The technical return of the cheque during its initial presentation does not negate the fact that the cheque was ultimately dishonored due to reasons attributable to the drawer. Shri Subrat Dash's refusal to refund the amount is not supported by legal principles, and the bank is well within its rights to initiate recovery proceedings under the Negotiable Instruments Act, 1881.

If Shri Subrat continues to deny his liability, OCUB can escalate the matter by:

a)   Filing a civil suit for recovery of the amount.

b)   Initiating criminal proceedings under Section 138 of the Negotiable Instruments Act for cheque dishonor, provided the legal conditions for such action are met.

* * *

WHEN CUSTOMERS CLAIM EXTRA DEPOSITS: THE FINE LINE BETWEEN POLICY AND REPUTATION

The Scenario

At the closure of operations at a sub-chest branch, the head cashier reported an excess cash of ₹50,000. The cashier was well experienced and was working as head cashier for the last 8 years. A detailed examination of the vouchers' denominational particulars revealed no discrepancies and the excess cash was thus credited to the branch's Sundry Deposits Account per banking protocol. Around closing time, as the manager Mr. Arun Singh was getting ready to leave, he was approached by Mr. Rajesh Mehta, the proprietor of Mehta & Sons, one of the bank's oldest and most valued customers.

Mr. Mehta stated that his cashier erroneously deposited ₹50,000 more during the deposit of ₹4,50,000 into their account. He claimed the records of his business in particular the cash book and daily transaction reports would prove the mistake. Mr. Mehta asked for an immediate refund of the excess amount so as to rectify the accounts.

This situation posed a challenging dilemma. Even though the claim seems reasonable, the bank is not obliged to return the amount merely on the basis of the customer's claim. Another claimant may appear in a day or two claiming the same amount. To solve these kinds of cases, the banks must follow the set procedure while ensuring that the interest of both the customer and the bank is intact.

The Challenge

In banking, cashiers often make errors in handling cash, and the result is excess/short cash balance during the day end, but please note its resolution is not easy. On one hand, the bank has to ensure that the funds are not released without checks and safeguards. On the other hand, the institution has to sustain its reputation to be dependable and trustworthy, especially to valued customers.

In this situation, Mr. Mehta's quick visit and offer to provide documents bolstered the seriousness of his claim. However, the branch had a responsibility to exercise due diligence to avoid potential disputes or financial liabilities arising from premature action.

Steps for Resolution

The following course will show how the branch can deal with the situation in a professional and fair manner:

1) Verification of Claim

Mr. Mehta's first step was to substantiate his claim by presenting relevant records, such as:

a) **Cash Book:** A detailed ledger showing daily cash inflows and outflows.
b) **Transaction Logs:** Evidence of the cash remittance, including the breakdown of denominations.
c) **Supporting Documents:** Receipts or any communication confirming the deposit.

At this stage, the role of the bank is to review these documents to check whether the excess remittance matches the declared excess of ₹50,000.

2) Indemnity Bond

If the verification proves the customer's claim to be right, the branch must ask Mr. Mehta to sign an indemnity bond.This legal instrument would protect the bank against:

a) Any future claims from third parties for the same amount.
b) Potential losses or liabilities arising from this transaction.

The indemnity must state that the customer will be solely liable for the refund and compensate the bank in relation to any claim/dispute.

3) Term Deposit Proposal

To reduce the risk further, the bank perhaps could ask the customer to convert the ₹50,000 into a term deposit for a year or more. This approach offers several advantages:

a) **For the Customer:** Mr Mehta earns the interest on the amount which balances the inconvenience.
b) **For the Bank:** The funds will be available to settle any claims that may arise in future and the bank is ready to settle disputes that may arise.

Given the customer's long association with the bank, the customer is likely to see it as a fair and mutually beneficial resolution.

4) Consultation with Controlling Authority

The branch should refer to its Controlling Authority for advice prior to settlement. This serves two purposes:

a) **Ensures Compliance:** Aligning with internal policies and regulatory frameworks.
b) **Provides Buffer Time:** Allowing sufficient time for any other claimants to come forward.

The consultation process not only strengthens the decision but also makes the resolution defendable at a later date.

5) Legal Considerations

It is important to note that the customer has a right to sue under the concept of "mistake of fact" as per Section 72 of the Indian Contract Act,1872 – which states that a party can recover money paid under a mistaken belief if he can prove the mistake.

For instance, if Mr. Mehta's office records prove that ₹5,00,000 was remitted instead of ₹4,50,000, he could claim the excess amount mistakenly remitted in the bank. The preparedness of the bank to counter such claims will fortify its position against risks.

Key Lessons for Bankers

1) **Always Verify Thoroughly:** All claims must be backed by authentic documents to avoid liability.
2) **Propose Balanced Solutions:** With innovative ideas like term deposits, the bank can address customer concerns and also protect itself.
3) **Understand Legal Frameworks:** Knowing the laws will help with compliance and decision-making.

Conclusion

Resolving Mr. Mehta's claim requires a delicate balance between safeguarding the bank's interests and honoring its commitment to customer satisfaction. If the branch follows a structured approach of verification, indemnity, term deposit, consultation, and speaking to legal advisers, a fair, and defensible resolution can be reached.

This case (or incident) shows just how complicated banking can be and the vital role professionalism and integrity can play in navigating them.

* * *

THE HIDDEN CLOCK: HOW LIMITATION PERIODS SHAPE LOAN RECOVERIES

The Scenario

On October 8, 2022, a term loan was sanctioned to a borrower for the purchase of a taxi. The repayment schedule contained monthly installments with the first one due on 08 November 2022. To comply with the same, the borrower issued a cheque dated 10 November 2022. The cheque was then presented for clearing on 12 November 2022 and was ultimately honoured and credited to the lender's account on 15 November 2022.

The last loan installment was due on 08 November 2025 but there were no further installments paid after the first installment. When will the limitation period for recovery start in such cases?

This case study digs into diverse situations affecting limitation period as per the Limitation Act, 1963, applicable banking law and relevant legal pronouncements.

Legal Framework

The Act Limitation Act 1963, governs the time limit within which the creditor can file a suit for recovery. Usually, the period of limitation concerning term loans is three years from the date on which the payment becomes due. But in specific situations, this period can get extended:

a) **Revival Letters:** Obtaining a standard revival letter signed by the borrower restarts the limitation period from the date of the latest revival letter.

b) **Acknowledgment of Debt:** Any written acknowledgment of the debt by the borrower within the limitation period also resets the timeline.

c) **Repayments:** The limitation period starts again from the day of making the last EMI or interest paid by the borrower.

Key Issue: Determining the Date of Payment

When a borrower issues a cheque, several critical dates are involved in the transaction:

1) **Date of the Cheque**: The date written on the cheque, indicating the intent to pay.
2) **Date the Cheque is Handed Over to the Bank**: The date the borrower submits the cheque to the lender.
3) **Date the Cheque is Lodged for Clearing**: The date the bank processes the cheque for collection.
4) **Date the Drawee Bank Pays the Cheque**: The date the funds are finally credited to the lender's account.

The key question is this: which of these dates are to be characterized as the date of commencement of the limitation period?

Legal Precedents

a) Courts have consistently held that the limitation period begins on the **date of the cheque**, provided the cheque is honored.
b) The reasoning is that the cheque reflects the borrower's intent to make the payment on the specified date. Subsequent delays in clearing or settlement do not affect the commencement of the limitation period.

Scenario Analysis

Scenario 1: Borrower Makes Timely Repayments

Assume the borrower pays the installments regularly through cheques issued on the installment due date. For example:

- First installment: Cheque dated **November 10, 2022**, paid on **November 15, 2022**.
- Second installment: Cheque dated **December 10, 2022**, paid on **December 14, 2022**.
- Final installment: Cheque dated **November 8, 2025**, paid on **November 10, 2025**.

In this case, the limitation period will start from the date of the last installment payment. The last installment payment was made on 10 November 2025. Therefore, the lender can initiate recovery any time within three years. That is, till 10 November 2028, the lender can begin recovery proceedings as long as there is no gap/default between installment payments.

Scenario 2: Borrower Defaults After Initial Payment

If the borrower pays only the first installment (as per original case), the limitation period would begin from the date of the first cheque, i.e., November 10, 2022. In this case:

- No revival letter is obtained.
- No subsequent payments are made.

The limitation period for recovery would expire on **November 10, 2025**. After 10.11.2025, the lender shall lose the right to enforce recovery unless the limitation period is extended by way of a revival letter or acknowledgment.

Scenario 3: Revival Letter is Obtained Annually

If the lender secures a standard revival letter from the borrower every year, the limitation period resets to three years from the date of the latest letter. For instance:

- Revival letter signed on **October 1, 2023.**
- Limitation period extended until **October 1, 2026.**

Even if the borrower defaults post-signing of the revival letter, the lender has the right to recover the loan till the date is extended.

Scenario 4: Cheque is Dishonored

If a cheque dated 10th Nov 2022 is bounced for insufficiency of fund, the limitation period – will not begin from the date of the cheque. Instead, the lender must take alternative steps.

1) File a complaint under Section 138 of the Negotiable Instruments Act, 1881 for cheque dishonor within 30 days of receiving the dishonor memo.
2) You may pursue recovery via a civil proceeding where the limitation would still begin from the first installment's due date, i.e. 8th November 2022.

Scenario 5: Part Payments After Default

Assume the borrower makes an irregular part payment on January 15, 2024, after defaulting for a year. According to the Limitation Act, the limitation period starts again from this part payment date. The lender's right to recovery is extended to January 15, 2027, even if no further payments are made.

Scenario 6: Loan Restructuring

If the loan is restructured on February 1, 2024, with a revised repayment schedule:

- The limitation period restarts from the due date of the first installment under the new agreement.
- For instance, if the first installment under the restructured loan is due on March 1, 2024, the limitation period would begin from that date.

Scenario 7: Borrower Acknowledges Debt Without Payment

If the borrower acknowledges in writing that he owes the loan outstanding amount on June 30, 2023, the limitation period shall restart from this date. The lender may then commence the recovery proceedings at any time until 30.06.2026, whether or not further payments are made.

Key Takeaways for Bankers

1) **Track All Payment Dates:** Maintain detailed records of cheques, revival letters and part payments for correct computation of the limitation period.
2) **Secure Revival Letters:** When revival letters are obtained on a regular basis, the limitation period gets extended thereby safeguarding the bank's right to recover.
3) **Use Legal Remedies Promptly:** In cases of cheque dishonor, file complaints under Section 138 of the Negotiable Instruments Act without delay.
4) **Monitor Loan Restructuring:** Confirm that the limitation period is properly reset on loan restructuring or rescheduling.

* * *

CASE STUDY 24

Navigating the Complexities of Set-Off Rights in Joint and Individual Banking Accounts: A Comprehensive Analysis

The Scenario

In a bustling town in Karnataka, two business partners, Mr. Ramesh Gowda & Mr. Shankar Shetty, held multiple banking accounts with their bank. Their financial arrangements included a mix of individual(self) and joint accounts, which often posed challenges when there are cases of liabilities that became overdue. The bank was faced with a situation to exercise the right of set-off - which is a banking principle to set off liabilities with the credit balance against their accounts.

The Accounts Involved

The following accounts were maintained by Mr. Ramesh Gowda and Mr. Shankar Shetty:

1) A savings bank account solely in the name of Mr. Ramesh Gowda.
2) An overdraft account held jointly in the names of Mr. Ramesh Gowda and Mr. Shankar Shetty.
3) A joint savings account held by Mr. Ramesh Gowda and Mr. Shankar Shetty.
4) An overdue loan account solely in the name of Mr. Shankar Shetty.

To resolve this tricky situation, the branch manager issued specific guidance to the newly appointed Probationary Officer regarding the use of the bank's set-off rights:

1) Set off the balance in Mr. Ramesh Gowda's savings account against the overdraft account held jointly with Mr. Shankar Shetty.
2) Set off the balance in the joint savings account against Mr. Shankar Shetty's overdue loan account.

3)   Set off the balance in the joint savings account against the joint overdraft account.

Is the Branch Manager correct?

This case study raises some very interesting issues of banking law and practicality over the exercise of the right of set-off in joint accounts and individual accounts.

Understanding the Right of Set-Off

The right of Set-off allows a banker to combine accounts and adjust the credit balance in one account against the debit balance in another account (i.e. adjusting the debts owed by the account holder). Although it is an uncomplicated principle when considering solely held accounts, there are complexities when we consider joint accounts or accounts with several signatures.

The set-off process is governed by:

1)   **The Indian Contract Act, 1872:** This act sets out the contractual obligations between bank and customers and defines the terms under which set off can be exercised.
2)   **wwReserve Bank of India (RBI) Guidelines:** RBI guidelines mandate fair & clear practices, including giving an account holder adequate notice before exercising set-off rights.

Analyzing the Case

1) Savings Account of Mr. Ramesh Gowda vs. Joint Overdraft Account

The bank proposed to use the credit balance in Mr. Ramesh Gowda's savings account to settle the overdraft in the joint account with Mr. Shankar Shetty. However:

a)   **Joint and Several Liabilities:** For a set-off to be valid in such cases, both account holders (i.e. Mr. Ramesh Gowda and Mr. Shankar Shetty) must be jointly and severally liable for the debt. If the overdraft agreement specifies individual liability for both partners, set-off might be permissible.
b)   **Consent Requirements:** The bank cannot utilize Mr. Ramesh Gowda's personal savings to settle the joint liability without his express consent.

His personal account is different from the joint liability unless he has agreed otherwise.

c)   **Legal Precedents:** Courts have consistently held that a personal account cannot be connected to a joint liability unless a direct contractual obligation exists.

Outcome: The bank cannot proceed with this set-off unless Mr. Ramesh Gowda consents to it or unless the overdraft terms clearly establish joint and several liabilities.

2) Joint Savings Account vs. Overdue Loan Account of Mr. Shankar Shetty

The manager suggested to the Probationary Officer that the balance in the joint savings bank account could be used to pay Mr. Shankar Shetty's overdue loan. This recommendation also poses significant legal and ethical challenges:

a)   **Nature of Joint Accounts:** A joint account is treated as a co-owned entity by all account holders together. Using the funds from the joint account to pay Mr. Shankar Shetty's sole liability would deprive Mr. Ramesh Gowda, a Joint account holder, of his rights as co-owner.

b)   **Explicit Consent:** The bank should get Mr. Ramesh Gowda's written permission before doing this set-off. Without such consent, the bank risks legal challenges for breach of fiduciary duty.

c)   **Regulatory Compliance:** The RBI has given guidelines to the banks that they must exercise set-off rights fairly & transparently, ensuring no co-owner is negatively affected without their agreement.

Outcome: The bank cannot set off the joint savings account balance against Mr. Shankar Shetty's overdue loan without explicit consent from Mr. Ramesh Gowda.

3) Joint Savings Account vs. Joint Overdraft Account

This is the most straightforward of the three proposed set-offs. The joint savings account & the joint overdraft account are held under the same names, and the liabilities are shared between both account holders.

a)   **Banker's Right:** In the absence of any express or implied agreement to the contrary, the bank has the right to set off the joint savings account balance against the joint overdraft liability.

b) **Notice Requirement:** According to RBI regulation, notice must be given to both account holders well in advance before a bank exercises this right. This ensures transparency and gives the account holders an opportunity to address the liability through other means.

c) **No Consent Issues:** Because the accounts are joint accounts, no further consent is required as long as the set-off is permitted by the account agreements.

Outcome: The bank may proceed with this set-off, subject to providing reasonable notice to both account holders.

Key Lessons for Bankers

a) **Understand Account Dynamics:** Always distinguish between individual & joint liabilities before exercising set-off rights.

b) **Ensure Consent and Notice:** Where necessary, obtain explicit consent and provide reasonable notice to account holders.

c) **Adhere to Regulatory Standards:** Abide by applicable laws and RBI instructions to prevent disputes and litigation.

* * *

CASE STUDY 25

THE HIDDEN PERILS OF LETTERS OF CREDIT AND BANK GUARANTEES – A CAUTIONARY TALE FOR BANKERS

Introduction

Letters of credits and bank guarantees are the key trade finance instruments facilitating smooth domestic and international transactions. They provide security to buyers and sellers, facilitating trust between parties. However, these non-fund-based facilities are subject to their own set of risks, which, if not managed adequately, may result in financial losses, frauds, and regulatory scrutiny.

This case study analysis discusses a scenario where a well-known Indian bank suffered a huge loss due to negligence in issuing an LC, thereby transforming the non-fund-based limit into a fund-based liability. It highlights the dangers, regulatory failures, and control standards that every banker must follow.

The Scenario: The Apex Exports Scam

Background

Apex Exports Pvt. Ltd., a leading textile trading company, had a long-standing relationship with Baroda Bank. The company frequently used LCs to import high-quality raw materials from overseas suppliers. Given its consistent track record of timely payments, Baroda Bank approved a non-fund-based LC limit of ₹100 crores, allowing Apex Exports to issue LCs within this sanctioned limit.

Apex Exports won an international order from a European client worth ₹200 crores for high-value textiles in early 2025. To fulfill this order, Apex Exports requested a ₹50 crore LC to import premium-grade cotton from an overseas supplier, TexSupplies Ltd., based in Hong Kong. Due to the urgency of the order and the company's past credentials, Baroda Bank granted the LC without any further security or due diligence.

Problem Statement: The Deception Unfolds

Initially, everything seemed to be in order. The LC issued by Baroda Bank in favor of TexSupplies Ltd. was dealt with according to the banking norms. The shipping papers were presented, examined on paper, and payments were made. However, as the due date for payment approached, Apex Exports suddenly started showing signs of financial distress. Apex Exports requested a short extension in time to make payment of their due obligations on account of a temporary cash flow mismatch due to delays in payment from their overseas buyers.

The bank did not find this request out of place and, given Apex Exports's long standing relationship with the bank, granted a 60 day extension without further ado. However, when Apex Exports failed to make payments after the expiry of the deadline, the first signs of trouble surfaced.

The First Suspicion – Delayed Buyer Payments or Something More?

Baroda Bank initially thought that it was the European buyer delaying the payments. However, when they went to check the claim, they saw that the buyer had already made full payments weeks ago! This contradicted Apex Exports' claim that their receivables were stuck. Where had the money gone?

Adding to the mystery, the money paid by the foreign buyer passed through a string of offshore accounts before disappearing into untraceable entities registered in Mauritius, the British Virgin Islands and other tax havens. It became evident that Apex Exports' promoters were siphoning funds rather than facing a genuine financial crunch.

The Second Shock – The Supplier Disappears

Meanwhile, the bank tried to get in touch with TexSupplies Ltd, the supplier in Hong Kong. Surprisingly, the supplier's email addresses bounced back, their office phone lines were disconnected, and their listed Hong Kong address belonged to a virtual office provider!

Sensing fraud, the bank initiated deeper scrutiny and collaborated with an international forensic audit firm. The shocking findings revealed that **TexSupplies Ltd. was a shell company with no history of actual trade transactions.** The so-called "shipment" did not exist. The Bills of Lading, invoices, and quality certificates were all **expertly forged** to create an illusion of a legitimate trade transaction.

The Domino Effect – A Series of Collapses

With this discovery, Baroda Bank immediately classified the LC as fraudulent exposure, but the damage had already been done. At the same time, the financial condition of Apex Exports worsened very fast and it defaulted on loans to other banks as well. Many other Indian banks that had given credit to Apex Exports suddenly realised that they could be exposed to huge NPAs.

Within weeks, the directors of Apex Exports resigned all together and fled the country, leaving behind debts exceeding ₹300 crore across multiple banks. A full-scale fraud probe was ordered by the CBI and ED.

The Final Twist – Insider Collusion Within the Bank

To the investigators' horror, some bank officials at Baroda Bank were found to have facilitated the fraud-

a) **LC Issued Without Standard Background Checks:** The Relationship Manager handling Apex Exports skipped important due diligence measures and went ahead with the approval of the LC (letter of credit) on the basis of a manipulated financial health report.

b) **Forged Email Correspondence:** Baroda Bank and TexSupplies Ltd emails were found to be fake. Furthermore, the internal staff of the bank colluded with the fraudsters to quickly allow payments.

c) **LC Transactions Not Recorded Properly:** Several of the fictitious letters of credit have not been properly approved, and internal audit logs have also been tampered with to avoid detection.

d) **Kickbacks and Bribery:** It was later discovered that certain bank employees were paid huge kickbacks to authorize all these transactions.

Regulatory Fallout and Legal Actions

Once the fraud was exposed, Baroda Bank's reputation suffered a massive hit. Due to repeated failures to conduct due diligence, the RBI imposed heavy penalties and summoned senior executives. As the siphoned money got tracked by investigators, international authorities were involved in looking for hidden funds in offshore accounts.

Several top executives from Apex Exports and the bank were arrested under The Prevention of Money Laundering Act (PMLA), 2002, and charged with criminal conspiracy under Sections 420 (cheating) and 120B (criminal conspiracy) of the Indian Penal Code (IPC).

Detailed Analysis: Where the Bank Went Wrong

The Apex Exports fraud at Baroda Bank was not a one-time oversight but a cascading failure of multiple banking processes, regulatory safeguards, and internal controls. While on the surface, it appeared to be a genuine trade finance transaction, deeper scrutiny revealed systemic weaknesses, negligence, and deliberate collusion that transformed a non-fund-based facility (Letter of Credit) into a full-fledged fund-based loss.

This section explores in detail the six major failures that led to Baroda Bank's exposure of ₹50 crores. These failures resulted in financial penalty, regulatory action and loss of reputation.

1) Liquidity Crunch and Devolvement of LC – A Missed Red Flag

At the core of the fraud was Apex Exports' liquidity crisis, which the bank failed to recognize in time.

How It Happened?

- Apex Exports was already having cash flow issues as seen with rising short-term borrowing and frequent delays in vendor payment.
- Instead of paying for its trade obligations from its own funds, the company continued issuing LCs, rolling over previous dues without an actual revenue inflow.
- When the LC matured, Apex Exports defaulted on payment, forcing the bank to settle the dues from its own accounts—turning a non-fund-based exposure into a direct financial hit.

Where the Bank Went Wrong?

- **Failure to Monitor Financial Health:** The Bank did not reassess the financial position of Apex Exports before issuing the LC of high value.
- **Ignored Frequent LC Devolvements:** The bank continued to issue new LCs to the company even though it had already defaulted on old LCs.
- **Did Not Cross-Check Customer Receivables:** The bank relied on Apex Exports' claim that payments from its buyers were delayed, instead of verifying with the buyers themselves.

How It Should Have Been Prevented?

- Using artificial intelligence for gauging risk, real time tracking of borrower's liquidity.
- Mandatory cash flow stress testing for large LCs before approval.
- Integration with external payment tracking systems to confirm incoming buyer payments.

2) Fraud by the Borrower – A Web of Deception

Apex Exports is guilty of fraud by abusing trade finance processes by using a loophole in LC verification.

How It Happened?

- Apex Exports worked with a fake supplier TexSupplies Ltd. to create false trade documents.
- The LC was taken against fraudulent invoices, which was later settled and the money siphoned off to offshore locations.
- As a result the company declared insolvent and the bank incurred a loss of ₹50 crore.

Where the Bank Went Wrong?

- **Did Not Verify the Supplier:** TexSupplies Ltd. had just been incorporated and thus had no trading history, yet the bank did not perform a supplier check.
- **Over-Reliance on Paper Documents:** The bank assumed that the presence of shipping invoices and Bills of Lading meant a legitimate trade took place.
- **Ignored Transaction Structuring:** The money received from the LC was routed through various tax havens. It is a typical indicator of trade-based money laundering (TBML).

How It Should Have Been Prevented?

- Design AI-backed trade fraud detection systems to identify high-risk counterparties.
- Enforce a "Know Your Supplier" (KYS) policy to verify the authenticity of overseas vendors.

- Use blockchain-based trade finance tracking to verify actual shipment movement.

3) Inadequate Security and Margin Requirements – A High-Risk Exposure

Baroda Bank did not mitigate risk by issuing this LC without adequate security and without margin deposit.

How It Happened?

- The bank only depended on past credit history and did not ask for any further security from Apex Exports.
- No security or personal guarantees were taken against even for a large-scale LC of ₹50 crore.
- When the LC devolved, the bank had no fallback option to recover its dues.

Where the Bank Went Wrong?

- **Failed to Demand a Cash Margin:** The bank issued the LC without requiring a security deposit so it ran the risk of losing 100% in case of default.
- **Did Not Enforce a Risk-Based Lending Policy:** High-value LCs should have required higher margins or additional guarantees.
- **Ignored Early Warning Signals:** The borrower's recent requests to increase their credit limit highlight possible distress.

How It Should Have Been Prevented?

- Set minimum cash margin requirement of 25-50% for high value LCs.
- Mandate corporate and personal guarantees for LCs above ₹10 crore.
- Monitor frequent LC limit hikes as a potential fraud indicator.

4) Supplier Fraud – Fake Shipment and Document Manipulation

The bank relied on **forged trade documents**, believing that goods were actually shipped.

How It Happened?

- The Bill of Lading was faked to evidence a non-existent shipment.
- The shipping company's stamp was forged, and the customs clearance papers were fake.
- Payment was made on the basis of these documents without verifying the arrival of the cargo.

Where the Bank Went Wrong?

- **No Physical Verification:** The bank failed to check with port authorities whether the cargo arrived.
- **Did Not Validate Bill of Lading with an Independent Source:** Fake Bills of Lading could have been detected through **global trade databases**.
- **Failed to Implement Documentary Consistency Checks:** The shipment was considered to be carrying textile raw materials but weight & volume discrepancies were ignored.

How It Should Have Been Prevented?

- Verify Bills of Lading with third-party shipping databases (International Maritime Bureau).
- Conduct surprise on-site checks for high-value LC transactions.
- Use smart contracts to ensure automated verification before payments.

5) Regulatory Lapses and Violation of Prudential Norms

The fraud exposed **multiple violations of RBI's prudential norms** for trade finance.

How It Happened?

- The LC was issued without compliance to RBI's risk management guidelines.
- Devolved LCs were parked in a separate account, hiding them from NPA classification.
- No Bill of Entry was submitted to prove that imports actually happened.

Where the Bank Went Wrong?

- Did Not Adhere to RBI's Prudential Norms on LC Issuance.
- Failed to Report LC Devolvements Accurately.
- Ignored ICAI's Audit Recommendations for Non-Fund-Based Limits.

How It Should Have Been Prevented?

- Mandate Bill of Entry submission within 90 days as per RBI guidelines.
- Ensure that all devolved LCs are classified correctly in NPA assessments.
- Conduct forensic audits for LC-backed transactions above ₹10 crore.

6) Insider Collusion Within the Bank – The Final Blow

Investigations later found that some bank officials were part of the fraud.

How It Happened?

- Emails between the bank and TexSupplies Ltd. were fabricated to fast-track LC approval.
- The bank's risk assessment reports were manipulated to clear the transaction.
- Certain senior officials received bribes to overlook red flags.

Where the Bank Went Wrong?

- No Internal Oversight on LC Approvals.
- Weak Whistleblower Protection Mechanism.
- Failure to Conduct Employee Background Screening.

How It Should Have Been Prevented?

- Implement independent risk oversight for LC transactions.
- Use AI-driven behavior analytics to detect unusual staff activity.
- Strengthen whistleblower protection to encourage fraud reporting.

Key Takeaways for Bankers – Checklist for Issuing LCs & BGs

1) Use Serially Numbered Security Forms to prevent unauthorized or fake guarantees as per IBA recommendations.

2) Large LCs must have two authorized signatures, with one from the Head Office or Controlling Office. LCs should include a column specifying sanctioning authority details.

3) Ensure all transactions are properly recorded in the books of the bank. However, strong internal control and periodical audit of LCs to avoid issuance of fraudulent or excess LCs.

4) Don't issue unsecured guarantees for large amounts by limiting exposure to unsecured commitments and preventing over-concentration in certain customer groups or industries.

5) Ensure Borrowers Have Adequate Payment Arrangements for LCs by verifying their ability to retire liabilities from their own funds or existing borrowing arrangements.

6) To avoid major financial risks, the guarantee exposure must be as per RBI standards.

7) Prohibit Misuse of Working Capital Limits by ensuring they are not used to settle capital asset purchase bills.

8) Before issuing letters of credit (LCs), check the trade history of the suppliers. Do your due diligence to check if they are genuine businesses and not just shell companies.

9) Ensure that Borrower's inventory levels of raw material LC are reasonable when compared to past historical levels & industry norms.

10) Always check whether the funds are blocked for the capital goods before issuing Letters of Credit to avoid defaults.

11) Adhere to the banking arrangements of the consortium, make sure you are issuing the LCs within the sanctioned limit and agreed bank shares and not exceeding the limits without the approval of the consortium.

12) Closely Monitor Non-Fund-Based Limits that convert into Funded Exposure to ensure that goods under devolved LCs remain under bank control or hypothecation.

13) Please make sure that the company submits the Bill of Entry of the Import LCs as per the RBI regulations within a period of 90 days to avoid fraudulent trade transactions and similar activities.

14) Preventing the Misuse of LCs by Bank Officials – Do regular reviews of LC Transactions to prevent their unauthorized issue, misrepresentation of documents and collusion with beneficiaries or others.

15) Limit Over-Reliance on Guarantees Without Due Diligence to ensure that borrowers do not over-reach their commitments based on guarantees.

16) When extending performance guarantees, be sure to examine the borrower's experience, financial capacity and ability to perform on the contract.

17) Ensure Full Compliance with LC Obligations by honoring all LC commitments to maintain trust and credibility in the trade finance system.

18) Take Strong Action Against Fraudulent Transactions by enforcing strict legal measures against fraudulent LC issuances, involving bank officials, and beneficiaries engaged in collusion.

* * *

CASE STUDY 26

THE HIDDEN RISKS OF AD HOC CREDIT: HOW FREQUENT SANCTIONS CAN LEAD TO DISASTER

Introduction

Ad hoc credit limits are temporary financial accommodations that banks provide to borrowers to address unforeseen liquidity demands. While these limits serve as a lifeline during emergencies, their frequent sanctioning can expose the bank to a myriad of risks. This case examines how repeated ad hoc sanctions by ICIC Bank to Global Tex Pvt. Ltd. triggered concerns over fund utilization, credit risks, and regulatory compliance.

The Scenario

Global Tex Pvt. Ltd., a mid-sized textile manufacturer based in Surat, Gujarat was engaged in the export of high-quality fabrics to clients in Europe and the Middle East. In 2024, the company had a working capital limit of ₹10 crore with ICIC Bank, which was meant to finance the company's operations and was backed by hypothecation of the company's inventory & receivables of ₹15 crore.

In March 2024, Global Tex was able to get a ₹25 crore export order from a UK retailer. To fulfill the order, the company requested an ad hoc credit limit of ₹2 crore, citing immediate procurement needs. The bank approved the request because the company had a good repayment history and good projected revenues.

However, over the next year, the company sought ad hoc sanctions six more times:

Month	Ad Hoc Limit Requested (₹ Crore)	Reason Cited	Approved?
March 2024	2.00	Bulk raw material purchase	Yes
June 2024	1.50	New export order	Yes
August 2024	2.50	Machinery repair and upgrade	Yes
October 2024	1.75	Cash flow mismatch	Yes
December 2024	3.00	Seasonal demand	Yes
February 2025	1.25	Delayed payment from buyers	Yes

Problem Statement

In early 2025, ICIC Bank, as part of its routine internal audit, flagged the Global Tex account over the following concerns:

1) **Frequent Ad Hoc Requests:** In a matter of one year, there were seven ad hoc sanction requests aggregating to ₹12 crore, which was 120% of the original working capital limit of the company.

2) **Non-compliance with RBI Guidelines:** All the mentioned ad hoc limits were not regularised within a period of three months as stipulated by the Reserve Bank of India (RBI).

3) **Insufficient Security:** The banks did not take any additional collateral for further ad hoc limits, thereby exposing themselves to recovery challenges.

4) **Lack of Fund Utilization Verification:** Evidence suggested fund diversion for purposes unrelated to the sanctioned objectives.

Detailed Analysis

1) Risk Indicators

A close examination of Global Tex's financials and transaction records revealed a number of potential risks:

a) **Diversion of Funds:** Some of the funds were transferred to a sister company that was not related to its textile business. For example, ₹1.2 crore from the sanction in August 2024 was sent to a company owned by the promoter's family.

b) **Cost Escalation:** The final cost to meet the export orders was 18 percent more than what was estimated, which indicates inefficiency. For instance, an order worth ₹25 crore required additional funding of ₹3.5 crore beyond the original budget.

c) **Inadequate Security:** While the initial working capital was backed by inventory worth ₹15 crore, subsequent ad hoc sanctions did not consider the decline in inventory turnover and receivable collection efficiency. By December 2024, the stock turnover ratio, which was previously 4.2, fell to 3.5 raising the risk of under-collateralisation.

d) **Irregular Account:** Frequent ad hoc sanctions, coupled with delayed repayments, led to irregularities. As of February 2025, ₹8 crore was the outstanding balance of sanctioned limits of which ₹4 crore is overdue by more than 60 days.

e) **Inefficient Fund Management:** The liquidity problem of the company indicated a greater operational problem. For example, receivables of ₹6 crore were overdue beyond 90 days which created liquidity stress.

2) Control Gaps Identified

ICIC Bank's audit revealed deficiencies in the sanctioning and monitoring process:

a) **Approval Lapses:** Any ad hoc limits over ₹2 crore should have been sent to the regional office for approval. However, branch-level authorities sanctioned all seven limits without seeking higher approvals.

b) **Inadequate Due Diligence:** The legitimacy of the company's claims for urgent funding was not verified by the bank. For instance, no independent valuation or market analysis was done to do an appraisal of the authenticity of the reasons cited for sanctions.

c) **End-Use Monitoring Failure:** There was no system in place to verify the actual utilization of the funds disbursed. While utilization certificates were provided by the company, these were not verified by anyone resulting in diversions by the company at will.

d) **Policy Non-Compliance:** According to the RBI norms, ad hoc limits must be regularized within 3 months. However, most of the sanctions remained pending for a long time, which showed a policy gap.

Proposed Solutions

To overcome these problems, the corrective measures taken by ICIC Bank are as follows:

1) **Strengthened Approval Mechanism:** Any ad hoc request that has more than ₹1 crore sanction amount should be sent to the regional credit committee for approval.
2) **Mandatory End-Use Monitoring:** An independent chartered accountant was appointed to certify the utilization of funds for all ad hoc limits above ₹50 lakh. Non-compliance would result in immediate withdrawal of the facility.
3) **Enhanced Risk Controls:** Borrowers with frequent ad hoc requests were flagged for detailed financial scrutiny, including cash flow analysis and reassessment of working capital requirements.
4) **Collateral Requirements:** Additional security or guarantees became mandatory for ad hoc limits exceeding 20% of the sanctioned working capital limit.
5) **Training and Awareness:** To improve compliance and better risk assessment, refresher training on RBI guidelines and internal credit policies was organized for Credit officers.

Impact

Within six months of implementing these measures:

a) The number of ad hoc sanctions was reduced by 40%.
b) Accounts flagged for irregularities due to ad hoc limits declined by 50%.
c) Loan recovery rates improved by 15 percent thanks to stricter collateral rules.

Global Tex's account was brought under control, with overdue amounts reduced from ₹8 crores to ₹3 crores which were supported by additional collateral worth ₹5 crore.

Key Learnings for Bankers

1) Strict Adherence to Guidelines:

It is imperative to comply with the directives of RBI with respect to ad hoc credit limits to avoid regulatory and financial risks.

2) End-Use Verification:

It's important to monitor the funds being utilized independently so that it does not deviate and are used for the stated objectives.

3) Strengthened Internal Controls:

A robust approval process & collateral requirements can mitigate risks posed to frequent ad hoc sanctions.

* * *

Cracking the Code: Risk Management in Heavy Cash Withdrawals – A Textile Trader's Mystery

Introduction

In early 2024, Catholic Bank, a reputed private sector bank in India, detected unusual cash withdrawal patterns from one of its working capital (WC) loan accounts. The account belonged to Sai Textiles, a Hyderabad-based wholesale textile trader. The firm, managed by proprietor Mr. Suresh Reddy, had availed a working capital loan of ₹15 crore to manage its day-to-day operations.

Although cash transactions are a common feature in some industries, especially in the unorganized sector, the high volume and unpredictability of the withdrawals raised suspicion. The bank's compliance team flagged the account after the borrower withdrew ₹12 crore in cash in three months which was not consistent with the borrower's pattern.

Working capital loans are meant to support a borrower's operational cycle by providing liquidity for inventory purchase, debtors' management, and other short-term needs. However, excessive cash withdrawals beyond operational requirements could indicate fund diversion, money laundering, or other fraudulent activities.

The Scenario

Sai Textiles mainly works in the states of Telangana and Andhra Pradesh supplying wholesale textiles to small retailers. The firm had a steady turnover of ₹50 crore annually, with consistent profit margins of 8–10%. In March 2024, during a standard compliance review, the Catholic Bank saw that there were cash withdrawals from the working capital account of Sai Textiles that had never been seen before.

From January to March 2024, the account recorded cash withdrawals as follows:

1) In January 2024, the total cash withdrawals amounted to ₹3.5 crore, with the highest single transaction being ₹50 lakh.
2) In February 2024, the total cash withdrawals increased to ₹4 crore, and the highest single transaction recorded was ₹60 lakh.
3) In March 2024, the total cash withdrawals further rose to ₹4.5 crore, while the highest single transaction reached ₹70 lakh.

In the past, Sai Textiles would withdraw cash of ₹1-1.5 crore per month, with no transaction more than ₹20 lakh. This sudden surge raised multiple questions.

Mr. Reddy, when contacted, explained that the withdrawals were for payment to unorganized suppliers, who insisted on cash. However, on a deeper look, this claim was found inconsistent.

Problem Statement

The main issue faced by Catholic Bank was whether the heavy withdrawal of cash by Sai Textiles was for the business or due to financial mismanagement or fraud. The bank faced the dual responsibility of safeguarding its asset quality while adhering to regulatory guidelines under the Reserve Bank of India (RBI) and preventing any potential misuse of funds.

The questions to address were:

a) Were the cash withdrawals justified based on Sai Textiles' business model?
b) Are the withdrawals connected to fund diversion or fraudulent activities?
c) How could the bank prevent such occurrences in the future?

Detailed Analysis

The bank initiated an extensive inquiry through a mix of data analytics, field checks and regulatory compliance.

1) Data Collection and Analysis

The audit team obtained transaction data from the bank's Core Banking Solution (CBS). This included:

a) **Cash Transaction Reports (CTR):** Highlighting high-value cash transactions.
b) **Exceptional Transaction Reports:** Spotting patterns that don't match account history
c) **Daily Cash Scroll Reports:** Verifying cash withdrawals at the branch level.

The data was exported in Excel month-wise and compared with a historical average. Key observations included:

a) The average monthly cash withdrawal in Q1 2024 stood at ₹4 crore as compared to ₹1.25 crore in 2023.
b) Withdrawal volume increased 220% compared to that of last year.

2) Verification of Business Profile

The auditors reviewed Sai Textiles' Know Your Customer (KYC) records and financial statements to validate the nature of its business. Key findings included:

a) **Sales Growth Stagnation:** Though the working capital needs were claimed to have increased, the sales of the firm remained flat at ₹12 crore in Q1 2024.
b) **Inventory Turnover Ratio:** Declined from 6x in 2023 to 4x in 2024, contradicting claims of increased operational activity.
c) **Profit Margins:** Reduced to 6% down from 10% indicating stress in financial operations.

3) Cross-Account and Related Party Analysis

The bank examined the accounts of related parties and associate entities linked to Sai Textiles. Findings included:

a) ₹2.5 crore was deposited into the account of Sai Enterprises, a firm owned by Mr. Reddy's brother.
b) Sai Enterprises' account had transactions not connected to textiles including purchase of property in Hyderabad.

This suggested possible fund diversion.

4) Borrower's Cash Book Review

The team requested Sai Textiles' cash book to check if the amount withdrawn is used for the intended purpose. Observations included:

a) Many entries for "Miscellaneous Expenses" without documentation.

b) High-value cash payments were labeled "supplier payments," but no matching invoices were provided.

c) Discrepancies in expense patterns compared to previous years.

5) Industry Benchmarking

Auditors compared the cash withdrawal pattern of Sai Textiles with peers. Findings:

a) Textile traders in similar markets conduct 70% of transactions digitally, leaving cash payments for small-value transactions.

b) Sai Textiles' cash-to-sales ratio of 33% was far higher than the industry average of 10–12%.

Bank's Control Measures

Catholic Bank put the following measures in place to fix the problem and stop it from future occurrence:

Preventive Controls

a) **Cash Withdrawal Limits:** Imposed a daily withdrawal cap of ₹25 lakh.

b) **Prior Approval Requirement:** Branch-level approval required for withdrawals beyond ₹10 lakh.

c) **Strengthened Working Capital Monitoring:** Required borrowers to submit monthly stock and debtor statements.

Detective Controls

a) **System-Generated Alerts:** Automated alerts for cash withdrawals over ₹5 lakh in one transaction.

b) **Concurrent Audit Reporting:** Regularly flagged unusual withdrawal patterns for management review.

Outcome

Sai Textiles was found to be involved in fund diversion. Specifically:

a) ₹5 crore from the loan account was redirected to Sai Enterprises for speculative real estate investments.

b) ₹3 crore was unaccounted for, with no verifiable end-use.

Catholic Bank classified the account as a Special Mention Account (SMA-2) as part of the RBI norms and took corrective actions:

a) Restructure the loan with enhanced coverage and tighter covenants.
b) Continuous monitoring of transactions for six months.
c) Legal proceedings to recover the misused funds.

Key Learnings for Bankers

1) **Robust Monitoring Mechanisms:** Leveraging technological alerts and CBS reports can lead to much earlier fraud detection.
2) **Cross-Account Analysis:** Related party transactions should be examined for diversion of funds.
3) **KYC and Business Profile Validation:** Updating borrower profiles regularly and benchmarking against industry peers is key to risk management.

* * *

HYDROPOWER OR FINANCIAL BLACK HOLE? A BANKER'S NIGHTMARE IN PROJECT LOAN MISMANAGEMENT

Introduction

In May 2015, RBI introduced the Red-Flagged Accounts (RFA) framework via its circular "Framework for dealing with frauds". The objective of this framework was to enable banks to identify Early Warning Signals (EWS) in loan accounts to facilitate fraud detection as well as to identify weaknesses. Among these signals, frequent changes in the scope of the project emerged as a serious risk, which caused cost overruns, delays in the project, fund mismanagement, etc. This case explores how Himalayan Hydro Ventures Pvt. Ltd., a Uttarakhand-based firm, faced scrutiny from Devbhoomi Development Bank, highlighting the critical role of vigilance and regulatory compliance in project financing.

The Scenario

The Hydro Power Project by Himalayan Hydro Ventures Pvt. Ltd.

In 2022, Himalayan Hydro Ventures Pvt. Ltd. (HHVPL) secured financing of ₹257.38 crore from Devbhoomi Development Bank for a 20 MW hydroelectric project in Chamoli, Uttarakhand. The project was assessed for completion in 4 years with an estimated total project cost of ₹312.54 crore. The promoters funded ₹55.16 crore in equity while the loan-to-value (LTV) was capped at 82%

The project had defined milestones such as the land purchase, necessary environmental clearances, and commencement of construction. The project was supposed to be halfway done by 2024. However, a number of issues cropped up when HHVPL suggested several modifications to the scope of work citing environmental hurdles and additional infrastructure.

Problem Statement

Frequent changes to the project scope, coupled with delays in execution and evidence of fund diversion, raised multiple red flags about the financial and operational integrity of HHVPL. The incident reveals the dangers to banks when the borrower does not follow the project plan and misuses the money.

Detailed Analysis

Timeline of Key Events

Date	Event
April 2022	Devbhoomi Development Bank sanctions ₹257.38 crore for HHVPL's hydroelectric project.
September 2023	HHVPL requests an increase in project outlay, citing environmental challenges.
November 2023	The bank approves a revised project cost of ₹393.87 crore and extends the DCCO to December 2025.
June 2024	HHVPL requests an additional ₹83.42 crore to add a second plant to the project.
August 2024	The bank's internal review uncovers fund diversion and minimal project progress.

Red Flags Identified

1) Frequent Changes in Project Scope

- HHVPL altered the scope twice in less than two years. The initial modification enhanced the project outlay by 26 percent, and the subsequent modification (inclusion of a new plant) took costs up further to ₹477.29 crore.
- The proposed changes were made without robust justifications or feasibility studies that were consistent with the project's appraisal.

2) Fund Diversion

- Bank audits revealed that ₹48.67 crore of the disbursed loan was used to settle debts in unrelated companies owned by HHVPL's promoters.
- Transfer of funds to vendors with suspected credentials further raised suspicion of collusion.

3) Delays in Project Execution

- By mid-2024, only 21% of the project was completed against the expected 50%. The acquisition of land & installation of equipment was significantly delayed.
- Reports indicated disputes with vendors, and several purchase orders were issued to small-time distributors instead of Original Equipment Manufacturers (OEMs).

4) Questionable TEV Study

- The Techno-Economic Viability (TEV) report for the revised scope was prepared by a lesser-known consultant. The report included multiple caveats and failed to address critical project risks.

5) Regulatory Non-Compliance

- When HHVPL filed its request for further funding, environmental clearances for the additional plant were still pending.
- The new plant was not backed by any cost-benefit analysis.

Bank's Actions

Enhanced Monitoring and Audits

Devbhoomi Development Bank decided to review the status and fund utilization of the project:

1) Site Visits and Independent Reports

- Repeated visits by the bank's staff have shown that no progress has been made.
- An independent engineer was appointed, who stated that the reported and actual progress didn't match.

2) Fund Flow Analysis

- The bank tracked fund flows & fund transfers to related parties amounting to ₹28.45 crore.
- Over ₹12 crore of expenses in the project were unaccounted for.

3) Compliance with RBI Guidelines

- The bank ensures compliance with the guidelines of the RBI Master Circular on Income Recognition, Asset Classification and Provisioning, before giving approval for changes in the scope.
- However, deviations in fund usage breach loan covenants.

Corrective Measures

1) Rejection of Additional Funding

The Bank rejected the request of HHVPL for ₹83.42 crore on account of misutilisation of earlier disbursements and lack of credible justification for the new plant.

2) Red-Flagging the Account

- The loan account of HHVPL was put under SMA-2 (Special Mention Account) indicating higher chances of default.
- The RBI's RFA framework flagged the account as possibly being a fraud.

3) Consortium Notification

- The bank shared its findings for the purpose of collective action with other lenders in the lending consortium.
- The matter was referred to CRILC (Central Repository of Information on Large Credits) for better supervision.

Outcome

By late 2024, Devbhoomi Development Bank had taken decisive steps to mitigate its exposure:

1) The bank began recovery proceedings for ₹257.38 crore by using the project assets as security.
2) The promoters of HHVPL have come under the scanner of the Fugitive Economic Offenders Act, 2018 for diversion of funds.
3) The consortium of lenders decided to enforce a forensic audit and pursue legal action against HHVPL.

Key Learnings for Bankers

1) **Independent Risk Team:** Set up an independent team for the project to assess the risk involved and make unbiased decisions, suitable for the bank.

2) **Robust Review Process:** Develop a detailed review process to assess scope changes for every project with respect to finance, technology and operations.

3) **Engage Reputed Agencies:** Work with credible agencies to carry out assessments of technical and economic viability to ensure reliability.

4) **Enforce Covenants:** Strictly enforce loan covenants to maintain control over the project's financial and operational aspects, with predefined consequences for breaches to address issues promptly.

5) **Monitor Progress and Fund Transfers:** It is important to continuously monitor the project's actual expenditures concerning the budget and also take a close look at fund transfers to catch issues early on and ensure that funds are not transferred without reason.

* * *

CASE STUDY 29

WHEN LIQUIDITY RAISES RED FLAGS: INVESTIGATING A LOAN REQUEST THAT DIDN'T ADD UP

Introduction

Banking involves more than just lending money—it demands a deep understanding of clients' financial motives and operations to mitigate risks and ensure that funds are utilized productively. A confusing scenario arises when borrowers seek substantial loans despite maintaining significant cash reserves. This case takes a look at a Goa-based businessman & provides an analysis of the red flags and risks bankers are likely to face.

The Scenario

Mr. Alvaro D'Souza, a prominent business owner in Goa, approached Konkan Cooperative Bank for a business development loan of ₹48.75 lakh at an annual interest rate of 12.25%. Mr. D'Souza's financial statements reflected cash and cash equivalents amounting to ₹1.08 crore. These funds were held in the form of current account balances, short-term fixed deposits, and marketable securities earning an average return of 7.85% per annum.

Given this liquidity position, the credit team at Konkan Cooperative Bank questioned Mr. D'Souza's rationale for incurring additional debt. In order to analyze the request, the team decided to evaluate if the request conformed with sound financial management, and that there was nothing unreasonable or any misuse of funds.

Problem Statement

Why would an over-liquid borrower apply for an expensive loan? Is the loan genuinely intended for business development, or does it mask underlying issues

140

such as fund diversion, fraudulent practices, or liquidity mismanagement? What should the bank do to confirm that the loan is necessary and appropriate?

Detailed Analysis

1) Examining Borrower's Financial Profile

Mr. D'Souza's financial records presented a mixed picture:

a) Cash and Cash Equivalents: ₹1.08 crore, comprising:

- ₹45 lakhs in a current account with Konkan Cooperative Bank.
- ₹38.75 lakh in short-term fixed deposits.
- ₹24.25 lakh in liquid mutual funds yielding around 7.85% annual returns.

b) Debt Position: Outstanding loans of ₹22.15 lakh from another nationalised bank, with an average interest rate of 11.75% per annum.

c) Business Performance: The business achieved an operating profit margin of 18%. Annual revenues stand at ₹6.4 crore & net profits at ₹1.15 crore.

The figures show that Mr. D'Souza's business was financially sound and liquid. Yet, the request for one more loan despite good reserves needed some investigation.

2) Cost-Benefit Analysis

The bank carried out an in-depth Cost Benefit Analysis(CBA) of the loan request:

a) Interest Cost of Borrowing: The loan will cost ₹5.97 lakh as interest expense annually at 12.25% per annum.

b) Opportunity Cost of Using Cash Reserves: Deploying ₹48.75 lakh from existing funds would reduce earnings from cash equivalents, which stood at an annual return of ₹3.82 lakh.

c) Net Cost Differential: Opting for the loan would impose an incremental cost of ₹2.15 lakh per annum.

This study found that it would be cheaper for Mr. D'Souza to use existing funds. Therefore, the bank needed to uncover Mr. D'Souza's motivation for incurring additional debt.

3) Financial Ratios and Indicators

The bank analyzed key ratios to assess the borrower's financial health & capacity to repay:

a) Current Ratio:

Current Ratio = Current Assets/Current Liabilities = ₹2.48 Crores/ ₹1.25 Crores = 1.98

A ratio of 1.98 suggested adequate liquidity to cover short-term obligations.

b) Debt Service Coverage Ratio (DSCR):

DSCR = Net Operating Income/ Total Debt Service = ₹1.28 Crores/ 28.12 Lakhs = 4.55

This strong DSCR indicated sufficient earnings to meet debt obligations.

c) Interest Service Coverage Ratio (ISCR):

ISCR = EBIT/ Interest Expense = ₹1.28 Crores/ ₹7.42 Lakhs = 17.26

The borrower's capacity to pay interest cost is very high as reflected in ISCR.

4) Investigating Cash Balances

The bank checked the cash reserves for their actual availability and use:

a)   **Consistency of Balances:** While the balances reported were large, they were very volatile during the month. On some days the current account balance has plunged to a low of ₹8.5 lakh, raising concerns over liquidity.
b)   **Extraordinary Transactions:** The sale of a non-core asset added ₹40 lakh to the company's inflows which may be temporary in nature.
c)   **Usage Patterns:** The discussions indicated that cash balance is earmarked for vendor payments, upcoming tax payments and reinvestment in mutual funds.

5) Early Warning Signals

Mr. D'Souza's borrowing behavior raised critical red flags with the bank:

a)   **Fund Diversion Risks:** There was no clear explanation for how the loan proceeds would be deployed to generate returns exceeding the borrowing cost.

b)   **Misrepresentation of Cash Balances**: The cash obtained from the sale of the asset temporarily inflated liquidity.

c)   **Lack of Financial Discipline**: The business did not seem to be backed by a strong cash flow management system but depended on intra-day balances and irregular inflows.

6) Borrower's Justification

During a detailed discussion, Mr. D'Souza offered the following explanations:

a)   **Backup Facility**: He wanted the loan as a contingency fund to maintain liquidity during unforeseen circumstances.

b)   **Expansion Plan**: The money would go towards expanding our business in South Goa which would require huge capital.

c)   **Vendor Payments**: A short-term loan would help tide over cash flow gaps that have arisen due to vendor payments which are due in the next 90 days.

Although these reasons appeared convincing, they did raise questions as to whether proper planning or clarity existed for spending the borrowed money.

7) Regulatory Compliance

To ensure compliance with the Reserve Bank of India (RBI) guidelines, the bank undertook the following measures:

a)   **End-Use Monitoring**: Konkan Cooperative Bank required documentation of the proposed utilization of funds along with contracts, invoices and project plan.

b)   **Borrower's Creditworthiness**: The lender analysed the credit history as well as the repayment pattern of the borrower which showed no default but some delays in loan servicing.

c)   **Assessment of Business Viability**: The bank assessed the sustainability of Mr. D'Souza's business model to see if future cash flows would allow him to repay the debt.

Key Learnings for Bankers

1)   **Early Warning Signals**: Investigate the need for borrowing when borrowers have significant cash reserves as it may leave scope for fraud.

2) **Cost-Benefit Analysis:** Make sure that borrowings are justifiable on the basis of individual needs and/or projects. Also, encourage them to use their own funds to save on interest costs.

3) **Financial Ratios:** Study key financial ratios such as the Interest Service Coverage Ratio, Debt Service Coverage Ratio and the like to assess the borrower's health.

4) **Current Ratio and Cash Flow:** Normally, a healthy and stable current ratio does not require new loans. Understanding the cash flow cycle of the borrower will determine the borrowing requirement.

5) **Genuine Funding Needs:** Make sure that the borrowings are based on genuine business requirements and not due to weaknesses of the financial discipline or accounting techniques.\

6) **Potential Red Flags:** Watch for red flags like fake cash balances, hidden cash covenants, and diversion of funds.

7) **Borrowing Purpose and Structure:** Ensure borrowings align with the borrower's core business objectives and consider the business structure for appropriate loan structuring.

8) **Data-Driven Decisions:** Use relevant data to verify that borrowings are necessary, will be used for business purposes, and can be repaid from cash flows.

Conclusion

After an extensive study, the Konkan Cooperative Bank sanctioned a reduced loan amount of ₹35 lakh with stringent monitoring. The bank mandated the submission of monthly cash flow statements, periodic utilization reports, and collateral enhancement. The measures ensured that the loan was genuinely needed, wisely used and sufficiently collateralised.

* * *

Case Study 30

The Double-Pledged Deception: How Borrowers Exploit Collateral Loopholes in Banking

Introduction

Collateral security is an essential safeguard in banking, providing a safety net for lenders in case a borrower defaults. It plays the role of an added layer of protection meant to act alongside the primary security (like inventory, machinery or receivables). Real estate, equipment, natural resources, and marketable securities are some of the commonly accepted forms of collateral. The value of the collateral is used to fix the limit of the loan to be sanctioned. The exclusive charge on collateral, as well as a clear title, is important because any ambiguity may expose the bank to huge credit and litigation risk.

To mitigate these risks, banks primarily take an exclusive charge over the security in such a way that there is no other lender claiming the rights over the same. However, in cases of consortium or multiple banking arrangements, banks may agree to share the charge in specific ways:

a) Pari-Passu Charge: All lenders share equitable rights in the collateral, in proportion to their outstanding exposure.

b) Second Charge: Only one lender has the right of recovery, while the rest can claim residual value only after the first lender's dues have been settled.

c) Equal Charge: The collateral value is divided equally among the lenders, irrespective of the loan amounts.

Even after these well-established frameworks, lots of times borrowers keep pledging the same collateral with different lenders without obtaining mandatory NOCs which leads to operational and financial difficulties. This case study examines one such instance involving a mid-sized textile company.

The Scenario

Background

RKG Textiles Pvt. Ltd., a long-time client of VSB Bank Ltd., specializes in fabric production and wholesale distribution. The company had a working capital limit of ₹39.75 crore. It sought enhancement of this limit to ₹59.82 crore to meet its ever-growing operational needs. As a part of the bank's due diligence, a full assessment of collateral and financial activities was done.

Initial Observations

a) **Collateral Details:** The firm has pledged a commercial property worth ₹25.47 crore & machinery worth ₹18.32 crore. The assets were necessary for the activities of the company and acted as a security for a large amount of loan.

b) **Turnover Discrepancy:** The company's annual turnover was ₹398.67 crore whereas bank statements had transaction activity of ₹191.82 crore. This raised many eyebrows regarding the accuracy of the reported figures.

c) **Unusual Financial Activity:** There was a sudden spike in high-value transactions of over ₹19.72 crore in the company's account. These transactions were not in line with the company's normal business.

Problem Statement

What can banks do to protect themselves from borrowers fraudulently pledging the same collateral to more than one lender, causing the value of the collateral to erode, leading to lawsuits & raising credit risk?

Detailed Analysis

A)Fraud Indicators

The following red flags pointed to potential fraudulent activities:

1) **Frequent Requests for Ad-Hoc Funds:** The borrower frequently sought temporary funding, citing unexpected cash flow mismatches.

2) **Rise in Cooperative Society Shares:** The balance sheet of the company shows an increase in shares of a cooperative society from ₹487 in Year 1 to ₹2437 in Year 3. Moreover, there were no financial activities cited on the balance sheet with respect to these shares.

3) **Delayed Mortgage Registration:** A delay by the borrower in mortgage registration suggested a possible manipulation of title deeds.

4) **Suspicious Transactions:** Sudden, high-value transactions, such as ₹19.72 crore & ₹21.34 crore, occurred without corresponding business activities.

5) **Undisclosed Loans:** The stock audit revealed the commercial property was pledged to a cooperative society for a loan of ₹12.18 crore, without an NOC from VSB Bank.

B) Stock Audit Findings

A stock audit that took place before the enhancement disclosed the following:

1) **Duplicate Collateral Use:** The commercial property provided as security was mortgaged with other lenders by the borrower, which violated the loan agreement of VSB Bank.

2) **Ownership Discrepancies:** The son of a director owned a residential property worth Rs 7.84 crore which was pledged as collateral. This asset was also pledged to a separate financial institution for a ₹3.62 crore loan.

C) Risk Analysis

1) **Credit Risk:** With the overlap of charges on collateral, the bank's exposure to unsecured credit increased considerably.

2) **Collateral Risk:** The marketability & recovery potential of the pledged assets were compromised.

3) **Legal Risk:** The existence of several claims on common collaterals complicated the legal proceedings & delayed the recovery.

Bank's Control: Prevention and Detection Mechanisms

VSB Bank adopted a number of preventive and detective controls to deal with these challenges:

A) Enhanced Verification Processes

1) Periodic Valuation of Collateral:

- Conducted bi-annual valuations to verify the current market value & ownership of pledged assets.

- Checked the property titles from the Registrar of Assurances for pre-existing charges.

2) Search Reports: Obtained detailed search reports from the Central Registry of Securitisation Asset Reconstruction and Security Interest of India (CERSAI) to verify existing charges on pledged assets.

B) Transaction Monitoring

1) **Behavioral Analysis:** Examined sudden spikes in account activity, including a single-day credit of ₹19.72 crore followed by withdrawals of ₹18.56 crore and ₹12.47 crore.
2) **Turnover Validation:** Detected mismatch between reported turnover of ₹398.67 crore vis-a-vis bank transactions of ₹191.82 crore.

C) Legal Safeguards

1) **Mandatory NOC Requirements:** Loan agreements were revised to mandate obtaining an NOC before creating any additional charges on collateral.
2) **SARFAESI Act, 2002:** Leveraged the SARFAESI Act to recover dues by selling the secured assets without judicial intervention.

D) Technology Integration

1) **Centralized Digital Registry:** Created an internal digital system that tracked collateral across branches and lenders on a real-time basis.
2) **AI-Based Surveillance:** Deployed AI tools to flag unusual financial patterns & discrepancies in borrower accounts.

Solution Implementation

A) Immediate Actions

1) **Loan Recall:** VSB Bank recalled the outstanding loan of ₹39.75 crore and froze further disbursements.
2) **Legal Proceedings:** Started recovery under the SARFAESI Act and lodged a complaint against the borrower regarding fraud.
3) **Forensic Audit:** Forensic auditors were hired to follow the funds and examine the authenticity of pledged assets.

B) Policy Revisions

1) **Stricter Loan Agreements:** The new clauses were introduced to charge penalties for not disclosing existing charges and for not obtaining NOC.
2) **Unified Consortium Framework:** Collaborated with other lenders to create standardized processes for collateral verification and charge registration.

C) Enhanced Monitoring

1) **Threshold-Based Audits:** Mandated asset and transaction audits for borrowers with credit facilities exceeding ₹20 crore.
2) **Transaction Surveillance:** By using the AI tools observed anomalies like consecutive high-value transactions.

Key Learnings for Bankers

1) **Understand Collateral Security** – Differentiate between **prime security** (main loan asset) & **collateral security** (backup asset used for recovery).
2) **Verify Collateral Ownership** – Before taking the collateral, please conduct a title check, a mortgage registration check and see that there are no other charges on the same title.
3) **Assess Acceptable Collateral Types** – Accept only real estate, machinery, stocks, bonds, or natural resources with clear ownership and market value.
4) **Charge Creation & Sharing:**

   a) **Exclusive Charge** – A single lender has full rights over the collateral.
   b) **Pari-Passu Charge** – Multiple lenders share equal rights over the collateral, based on outstanding loan ratios.
   c) **Second Charge** – The first lender has primary rights; the second lender can claim only residual value.
   d) **Equal Charge** – The collateral is divided equally among all lenders.

5) **Identify Fraud Indicators** – Look out for borrowers pledging the same collateral to multiple lenders, fake documents, and unusual financial activities.

6) **Assess Risks** – Evaluate credit risk (borrower repayment ability), collateral risk (market value decline), legal risk (disputed ownership), & fraud risk (misuse of security).

7) **Monitor Transactions & Financials** – Regularly review borrower's financial statements, account activities, and mortgage registrations for anomalies.

8) **Implement Preventive Controls** – Conduct periodic collateral verification, stock audits, legal checks, and ownership confirmations to prevent fraud.

9) **Follow Audit Best Practices** – Ensure search reports, due diligence, and fraud indicators are properly reviewed and acted upon in line with banking policies.

* * *

Stock Statements or Smoke Screens? When Stock, Debts, and Creditors Tell Different Stories

Introduction

In modern banking, working capital financing is a lifeline for businesses, allowing them to operate seamlessly by funding short-term assets such as stock & receivables. In order to offer these facilities, banks generally rely on primary securities like stock and book debts and ask for periodical stock statements from the borrower. The statements play an important role in analyzing the financial health, operating efficiency & compliance with credit norms. Any difference in these statements indicates inefficiencies, mismanagement or fraud.

This case study examines Rajasthan Specialty Chemicals Ltd., a considerably well-known manufacturer, and focuses on the abnormalities of stock movements, which certainly raise some serious red flags. The study emphasizes the necessity of thorough stock analysis and effective risk management practices for the bankers.

The Scenario

Company Background

Rajasthan Specialty Chemicals Ltd. (RSCL) is based in Jaipur & specializes in the production of specialty chemicals used in agriculture and pharmaceuticals. The company operates with a well-defined production cycle of 3 to 4 days & reports a gross profit margin of 24.8%. RSCL has an annual turnover of ₹52.3 crores and has been availing working capital finance of ₹8 crores from Marwar Cooperative Bank Ltd. (MCB), secured by stock and book debts.

The company is consistent in submitting monthly stock statements & claims compliance with all regulatory and operational norms. However, a routine review of the stock statement raised flags about the Work-in-Progress (WIP) and the movement of stock, book debts and trade creditors.

Stock Statement Summary

The following data captures the movements in stock, book debts, & trade creditors for the month of **October 2024**:

a) **Stock:** Opening balance was ₹102.5 lakh, with ₹34.7 lakh added and ₹41.3 lakh deducted, closing at ₹95.9 lakh.

b) **Book Debts:** Opened at ₹153.8 lakh, saw ₹58.3 lakh added and ₹96.2 lakh deducted, closing at ₹115.9 lakh.

c) **Trade Creditors:** Started at ₹82.4 lakh, with ₹12.5 lakh added and ₹52.7 lakh deducted, closing at ₹42.2 lakh.

Observations

1) **Discrepancy in WIP:** The company reported WIP between ₹2.05 crore to ₹2.43 crore which is much higher than the expected range of ₹0.30 crore to ₹0.42 crore in production cycle.

2) **Book Debts Anomalies:** The total increase in book debts was ₹58.3 lakh as against the expected amount of ₹45.43 lakh (stock deductions plus 10% profit margin).

3) **Stock-Creditor Misalignment:** Despite consumer stock rising by ₹34.7 lakhs, trade creditors went up by just ₹12.5 lakhs. This indicates that the Company does not pay its suppliers promptly.

Problem Statement

Why do the reported WIP values, book debts, & stock movements deviate significantly from RSCL's typical production & operational model? Could these anomalies signify inefficiencies, intentional misrepresentation, or potential fraud?

Detailed Analysis

1) Work-in-Progress (WIP) Discrepancy

- **Reported WIP:** ₹2.05–₹2.43 crores.
- **Expected WIP:** For a 3–4 day production cycle and a gross profit margin of 24.8%, the WIP should range between ₹0.30 crores and ₹0.42 crores.

Analysis:

a) The WIP figure shows that stocks are likely to be in process for 18–20 days which is much longer than the usual cycle.

b) Possible reasons:

- Overstated WIP to inflate working capital requirements.
- Delays in converting raw materials to finished goods.
- Incorrect classification of finished goods as WIP.

2) Book Debts Anomalies

Key Figures:

a) Stock Deductions: ₹41.3 lakhs.
b) Expected Book Debts Addition: ₹45.43 lakhs (₹41.3 lakhs + 10% margin).
c) Actual Book Debts Addition: ₹58.3 lakhs.

Analysis:

The additional 12.87 lakhs in book debts could mean:

a) Inflated sales figures to secure additional credit.
b) Delayed payments from debtors.
c) Unrecorded cash collections.

3) Stock-Creditor Misalignment

Key Figures:

a) Stock Additions: ₹34.7 lakhs.
b) Trade Creditors Additions: ₹12.5 lakhs.

Analysis:

The difference of ₹22.2 lakhs suggests:

a) Direct procurement from cash resources rather than credit.
b) Underreporting of trade creditor liabilities to project healthier financials.
c) Possible diversion of funds to other uses.

4) Risk Indicators

The following red flags were identified:

a) **WIP Discrepancies**: Misalignment with production cycles suggests inefficiency or misrepresentation.

b) **Inflated Book Debts**: Excess additions may be a sign of late collections or fake sales.

c) **Stock-Creditor Gap**: Misalignment indicates discrepancies in procurement & payment practices.

Bank Follow-up Process

The bank initiated audit based on the following sources:

a) **Stock Statements**: Data submitted by RSCL was scrutinized for consistency.

b) **GST Returns**: Cross-verified stock movements against sales tax records.

c) **Excise Records**: Analyzed excise filings for production and sales figures.

d) **Tax Audit Reports**: Examined to identify inconsistencies in reported financials.

Key Findings

1) There was discrepancy in the stock additions and the GST Returns with the likely objective of under-reporting.
2) Delayed debtor payments were evident from aging reports.
3) Excise record shows mismatch in production and raw material consumption.

Bank's Control Measures

1) Automating Stock Analysis

Implementing systems to detect anomalies, such as:

a) Disproportionate WIP values.
b) Misaligned stock-to-creditor movements.
c) Unusual debtor additions.

2) Enhanced Reporting Requirements

Mandating detailed stock statements, including:

a) Breakdown of raw materials, WIP, & finished goods.
b) Movement of book debts & trade creditors.
c) Justifications for significant deviations.

3) Periodic Audits

Conducting quarterly audits to:

a) Cross-verify stock data with GST and excise filings.
b) Analyze debtor aging & cash flow statements.
c) Validate procurement records against trade creditor movements.

Borrower Engagement

The bank engaged RSCL's management to:

a) **Clarify Anomalies**: Clarify overvalued work-in-progress values & fluctuating stock transfers.
b) **Improve Operational Efficiency**: Reduce production delays & align WIP with the production cycle.
c) **Enhance Reporting Accuracy**: Put internal controls in place for precise and transparent reporting.

Key Learnings for Bankers

1) **Detailed Stock Analysis is Crucial**: Regularly analyzing stock statements can expose inefficiencies, mismanagement, or fraud.
2) **Cross-Verification is Essential**: Check validity of stock data with the help of external documents like GST returns, excise returns, tax filings, etc.
3) **Proactive Risk Management**: Automate your anomaly detection for early detection and corrective actions.

* * *

THE HIDDEN HAND: HOW RELATED PARTY TRANSACTIONS CAN SINK A BUSINESS—AND ITS BANK

Introduction

Interconnected companies often engage in transactions that can blur the lines between genuine business dealings & financial manipulation. While these kinds of transactions look like business as usual, they often hide dangers such as liquidity crises, diversion of funds, & inflation of profits. The case study elaborately explains the situation of Stellar Industries Ltd. and its subsidiaries financial practices. The analysis delves into the risks for the lending bank, compliance with laws, and mitigating strategies.

The Scenario

New Global Bank, an established Indian private-sector bank, conducted a routine credit review of one of its long-standing corporate clients, Stellar Industries Ltd. Stellar Industries, a mid-sized manufacturer with ₹412.56 crore of annual revenue, was very dependent on its group companies for business operations. Its corporate structure included four subsidiaries & two sister concerns, all engaged in various stages of the manufacturing and distribution process.

Key Observations

a) **Revenue Concentration:** Sales to its subsidiaries contributed approximately ₹259.87 crore (63% of total revenue).

b) **Receivables Spike:** Receivables from interconnected companies grew sharply from ₹71.34 crore in 2022 to ₹112.48 crore in 2024 with minor recovery.

c) **Fund Diversion:** Stellar borrowed ₹98.47 crore at an interest rate of 8.25% but lent ₹62.78 crore to its sister concerns at 4.50%, well below market rates.

These findings raised red flags over the financial conduct and health of Stellar Industries, leading New Global Bank to launch a full scale investigation.

Problem Statement

The bank faced multiple critical issues:

a) Were Stellar's transactions with its interconnected companies conducted at **arm's length,** as mandated by law?

b) Did the high receivables and fund diversion indicate a liquidity or solvency risk?

c) Were the transactions real or simply book entries that were used to inflate profit and asset figures?

d) What protective measures could New Global Bank take to reduce group-level financial risks?

Detailed Analysis

Nature of Transactions

Stellar Industries' financials showed many intra-group transactions like:

a) Sales of raw materials and finished goods to its subsidiaries.

b) Advances and loans extended to sister concerns.

c) Service charges and management fees billed to interconnected companies.

These transactions were ₹282.69 crore or almost 68.5% of Stellar's total business.

Arm's Length Pricing

A critical step of the investigation was to find out whether the transactions were at a fair price as required under Section 188 of the Companies Act, 2013. The findings were concerning:

a) **Sales Pricing:** Stellar sold its primary product, high-grade steel sheets, to subsidiaries at ₹38,900 per metric ton, compared to ₹42,500 per metric ton charged to third-party customers.

b) **Interest Rates:** The Company has given loans to its sister concerns at the 4.50% interest rate as against 9.75% market rate.

The difference in pricing and interest rates indicate possible favoritism & procedural violation of arm's length.

Financial Implications of Fund Diversion

Stellar's financials showed that:

a) Around ₹62.78 crore was diverted as loan to its sister concern, which together earned a net profit of only ₹3.24 crore in 2023.
b) The loan repayment plan was not clear as they had no timeline or terms to repay.
c) Stellar had a cost of funds of 8.25%. These rates being charged by the company were below market rates and resulted in a net loss of ₹2.34 crore annually.

Liquidity and Solvency Risks

The increasing receivables from interconnected companies were a significant red flag:

a) Receivables Trend:

- 2022: ₹71.34 crore
- 2023: ₹91.67 crore
- 2024: ₹112.48 crore

b) Days Sales Outstanding (DSO): Stellar's related parties' Days Sales Outstanding (DSO) was 184 days compared with 91 days for the industry average.

The liquidity of stellar was affected by increased payment cycles which in turn raised concerns about its ability to meet short-term obligations.

Group-Level Concentration Risk

New Global Bank consolidated the financials of Stellar Industries & its interconnected entities to assess group-level health. Key metrics revealed:

a) **Group Revenue:** ₹718.24 crore
b) **Group Debt:** ₹273.89 crore
c) **Debt-to-Equity Ratio:** 2.37 (industry average: 1.75)

The significant debt levels and revenue concentration with the group created critical risks if one of the entities went bust.

Compliance with Laws and Regulations

Stellar's transactions were examined with respect to Section 188 of the Companies Act concerning related party transactions:

a) **Board Approval:** While Stellar obtained board approval for transactions, detailed records were incomplete.
b) **Shareholder Resolution:** No special resolution was passed, as required by law, for any transactions that exceed 25% of company turnover.
c) **Fair Pricing:** Pricing of transactions was not at arm's length and was not at fair market value.
   Non-compliance with these provisions exposed Stellar to regulatory penalties & reputational risks.

Economic Rationale

The bank was also scrutinising whether there was any business purpose for the transactions:

a) **Operational Needs:** The transactions seemed more motivated by financial adjustments than by operational need.
b) **Fund Diversion:** Loans to sister concerns were used to cover operational losses rather than for growth or expansion.

Trend Analysis

To identify patterns, the bank analyzed historical data:

a) **Outstanding Receivables:** Rose by 57.7% in two years with few recoveries.
b) **Profitability:** Stellar's net profit margin went down from 12.4% in 2022 to 8.7% in 2024 as receivables & interest costs rose.

Mitigation Measures

Global Bank was able to lessen its risks in several different ways:

a) **Demand for Guarantees:** The bank obtained corporate guarantees from Stellar parent company, Stellar Holdings Ltd., which had a good credit rating and net worth of ₹156.32 crore.
b) **Transaction Monitoring:** A covenant was introduced requiring quarterly disclosures of related party transactions & cash flows.

c) **Risk-Based Pricing:** The higher risk profile of Stellar prompted the bank to change its interest rate to 9.50% from 8.25%.

d) **Revised Loan Terms:** Stellar was required to shorten the repayment terms of intra-group loans and base them on industry standards.

Key Lessons for Bankers

1) **Ensure Transactions Are Conducted at Arm's Length Pricing:**

   Check that all transactions are based on market pricing and free from preferential treatment to avoid conflicts.

2) **Validate Underlying Business Rationale:**

   Evaluate whether transactions are vital for the conduct of a business or whether they have merely been structured to misrepresent financial results, evade tax or inflate turnover.

3) **Monitor Large Outstanding Balances & Receivables:**

   Thoroughly analyze the amounts that are outstanding to see if they are indicative of any genuine trade relationships.

4) **Identify Signs of Profit Inflation or Asset Overvaluation:**

   Ensure that the transactions do not involve artificial profit booking, stock transfers, dummy sales, etc. to inflate the financials.

5) **Analyze Trends in Intra-Group Transactions:**

   Analyze past transaction trends to see whether there are any spikes, drops or changes happening suddenly that may show financial stress or fraud.

6) **Assess Risks of Fund Diversion via Inter-Company Transfers:**

   Verify whether fund movements (loans, advances, capital transfers) are genuine business transactions or being used for unauthorized diversions.

7) **Check for Double Financing Risks in Working Capital Assessment:**

   Exclude inter-group transactions when calculating working capital needs to prevent financing the same transactions multiple times.

8) **Obtain Financials for All Interconnected Entities:**

Evaluate the consolidated financial position of the entire group to understand exposure risks & ensure no hidden liabilities.

9) **Evaluate Inter-Group Lending and Borrowing Practices:**

Intra group loans must have the right interest rates, the right structure and documentation and must not give any entity an undue advantage.

10) **Review Loan Repayment Guarantees and Credit Support Mechanisms:**

Seek cross guarantees or financial backstops from group entities with stronger financials to mitigate default risks.

11) **Assess NPA & Default Risks from Large Outstanding Transactions:**

Make sure to check for provisioning, NPA classification, or write-off of loans due to long out standings.

* * *

Case Study 33

The SME Growth Trap: When Expansion Masks Hidden Financial Risks

Introduction

Mr. Gopalakrishnan is the Branch Manager of Mahatma Nagar Branch of Kaveri Grama Bank at Coimbatore who is managing a portfolio of ₹532.25 crores out of which advances are ₹256.47 crores. The branch has a significant focus on regional trade, as evidenced by advances in SME of ₹137.89 crores. A partnership firm, Sri Krishna Traders, recently put up a proposal before him. The company was looking to transfer the existing limits from another bank & also requesting an enhanced limit.

Sri Krishna Traders is a rapidly growing player in the wholesale distribution of imported electronic gadgets, particularly mobile phones. While their business growth looks promising, certain red flags emerge regarding their financial practices, governance, and market dependencies. This case study explores the due diligence process necessary to evaluate the proposal while weighing the risks and opportunities for the bank.

The Scenario

Background of Sri Krishna Traders

Sri Krishna Traders is a partnership firm established on 10th March 2015 and trades in mobile phones imported from foreign vendors mainly from mainland China. Key suppliers include Z-Tech Solutions, Chinotel Inc., & XiXo Electronics, with products ranging from ₹2,950 - ₹7,250 per handset. These mobile phones are sold to dealers across Tamil Nadu, Kerala, Karnataka, & Andhra Pradesh.

Under Mr. Anand Raj (key promoter) & Mr. Venkatesh Babu (silent partner), the firm has shown steep revenue growth.

a) In 2015-16, sales were ₹27.45 crore, net profit stood at ₹2.17 crore, and closing debtors were ₹4.92 crore.

b) In 2016-17, sales increased to ₹56.32 crore, net profit rose to ₹4.18 crore, and closing debtors reached ₹7.68 crore.

c) By 2017-18, sales peaked at ₹82.89 crore, net profit grew to ₹6.12 crore, and closing debtors stood at ₹10.45 crore.

Although it is on an upward trend, the operations of the firm are highly concentrated among five suppliers that account for 78% of purchases, & eight retailers make nearly 72% of sales.

Banking and Financial Details

Sri Krishna Traders currently has a cash credit limit of ₹4.72 crores along with a letter of credit (LC) facility of ₹2.17 crores provided by Chennai Cooperative Bank, secured by Mr. Babu's personal property worth ₹9.42 crores. They now seek to shift these facilities to Kaveri Grama Bank and enhance their limit to ₹7.15 crores (cash credit) and ₹3.29 crores (LC).

They provided the unaudited financial statements for FY 2023-24, three years GST returns, & a stock statement showing stock of ₹12.89 crores. Ironically, their bank account statement showed frequent overdrafts.

Problem Statement

Can Kaveri Grama Bank sanction the enhanced credit facility for Sri Krishna Traders while ensuring financial soundness, and mitigating operational risk? What qualitative and quantitative analyses should guide this decision?

Detailed Analysis

A) Qualitative Appraisal

1) Promoter Background

a) **Mr. Anand Raj:** At 49, he has 30 years of trading experience but a record of constantly switching businesses (six in total). His last business closed abruptly, raising concerns about his financial discipline.

b) **Mr. Venkatesh Babu:** A passive partner who puts up collateral but does not get involved in day-to-day activities. He owns multiple ancestral properties.

Concerns:

a) Mr. Raj stays in rented accommodation although he claimed huge past profit.

b) No collateral input from Mr. Raj although he is an important man of the firm.

Recommendations:

a) Get verified records of Mr. Raj's history of financial investments and liabilities.

b) Insist on getting more collateral from Mr. Raj to align interests.

2) Business Model Vulnerabilities

a) Overdependence on a narrow vendor and customer base heightens concentration risk.

b) Recommendation: Diversify the supplier base and customer portfolio. Obtain reports on major suppliers and buyers.

3) Market Risks

a) Mobile trading is highly susceptible to technological obsolescence & price volatility.

b) Recommendation : Include a conservative margin while appraising inventory and receivables.

B) Quantitative Appraisal

1) Financial Performance

a) The annual sales for FY 2017-18 were 82.89 crores. Of this, 2.19 crores were not routed through bank.

b) Recommendation: Reconcile the difference by checking the cash books of the firm & getting the same verified by the external auditor.

2) Security Coverage

a) Primary Security:

–   Inventory: ₹12.89 crores

–   Receivables (<6 months): ₹8.25 crores

b) Collateral: ₹9.42 crores (Mr. Babu's properties)

c) **Recommendation:** Conduct physical verification of inventory and validate the receivables list for age and genuineness.

3) Banking Conduct

a) There were multiple overdrawn instances in Q1 FY 2017-18, exceeding sanctioned limits 4 times.

b) Recommendation: Assess repayment discipline, cheque returns, & adherence to statutory dues.

4) Financial Ratios

a) Current Ratio: 1.32 (indicating borderline liquidity).

b) Debt-to-Equity Ratio: 3.45 (indicating high leverage).

c) Recommendation: Use tighter repayment schedules, escrow arrangements and similar terms for risk mitigation.

5) GST and Statutory Compliance

a) GST returns matched the reported sales, confirming transaction legitimacy.

b) Recommendation: Check timely deposit of TDS, GST, & employee salary payments.

Regulatory and Risk Checks

a) **Credit Bureau Data:** Analyze CIBIL reports for past defaults.

b) **Regulatory Compliance:** Ensure compliance with RBI Master Directions related to lending to small and medium enterprises (SMEs) including prudential norms on exposure limits.

c) **Third-Party Validation:** Utilize MCA records and outside credit reports for financial validation.

Decision Framework

Using the **5 Cs of Credit**, the proposal's assessment yields the following insights:

Parameter	Assessment	Recommendation
Character	Moderate (business shifts)	Detailed inquiry into past ventures.
Capacity	Adequate (consistent profits)	Focus on liquidity and receivable management.
Capital	Weak (no collateral from key promoter)	Demand personal collateral from Mr. Raj.
Collateral	Sufficient (₹9.42 crores)	Verify property titles & conduct revaluation.
Conditions	Moderate (sector risks)	Conservative credit terms & stock audits.

Recommendations

1) Approve the facility with stringent conditions:

   a)   Collateral contribution from Mr. Raj.
   b)   Escrow mechanism for receivables.
   c)   Mandatory stock and receivables audits.

2) Monitor key risks:

   a)   Technological obsolescence.
   b)   Market diversification.

3) Reassess the firm's creditworthiness biannually.

Key Learning Checklist for Bankers

1) Verify Promoter's Financial Integrity:

   a)   Assess why a profitable promoter is not investing in real estate or assets.
   b)   Collect documentary proof of investments and asset ownership.

2) Collateral Security Justification:

   a)   When the promoter is not offering collateral in spite of profitability, investigate.
   b)   b) Insist on some collateral from the key promoter to mitigate risk.

3) Supplier & Customer Reputation Check:

Get inputs from suppliers, customers, and credible industry sources on the promoter's credibility.

4) Cross-Check Cash Flow with Bank Credits:

a) Make sure that total summation of credit in the bank aligns to sales disclosed. (GST v/s bank credits)

b) Investigate discrepancies in cash realization.

5) Verify Statutory Dues Payments:

a) Make sure to make timely payments of TDS, GST, PF & salaries via bank payment.

b) Delay or non-payment may indicate financial stress.

6) Analyze Credit Utilization & Account Conduct:

a) Monitor CC limit usage, cheque returns, penal interest charges, & overdue amounts.

b) Frequent excess utilization is a red flag.

7) Stock Statement vs. Balance Sheet Verification:

a) Cross-check stock statements with the balance sheet & physical verification at the godown.

b) Ensure reported stock matches reality to prevent fraud.

8) Debtors & Creditors Scrutiny:

a) Validate that the names in the debtor/creditor list match with account statements.

b) Check the age-wise breakup—outstanding dues over six months should be examined closely.

9) MCA, CIBIL, and RBI Default List Check:

a) Conduct a thorough background check via MCA website, Probe 42, & CIBIL.

b) Look for any RBI willful defaulter listing.

10) Net Worth & Capital Movement Verification:

a)   Gather and evaluate the promoter's net worth information with documents.

b)   Investigate capital movement patterns in business.

11) Nature of Business & Compliance Check:

a)   Ensure that the nature of goods mentioned in GST returns is the same as the actual business of the firm.

b)   Watch out for undisclosed diversification or unrelated transactions.

12) Thorough Financial Ratio Analysis:

a)   Using provisional & audited financial statements assess profitability, liquidity & leverage ratios.

b)   Discrepancies in financial health should prompt deeper scrutiny.

By addressing these factors, Kaveri Grama Bank can make an informed decision that balances business growth with financial prudence.

* * *

CASE STUDY 34

WHEN TRUST BACKFIRES: THE HIDDEN DANGERS OF CONSORTIUM LENDING

Introduction

M/s SteelTrack Ltd., a public limited company incorporated in 2019, gained prominence in the iron and steel trading industry in North India. With an experienced management team and an impeccable growth trajectory, SteelTrack Ltd. became a reliable client for Pioneer Bank Ltd. by 2020. Banking on its consistent performance, Pioneer Bank led a consortium of financial institutions to provide substantial credit facilities for the company's ambitious foray into steel manufacturing in 2024.

But, what began as a wholesome effort to set up a state-of-the-art steel plant transformed into a financial disaster revealing systemic lapses in credit monitoring & regulatory non-compliances. This case examines the events leading to the downfall, revealing the dangers of lax oversight & the misuse of banking facilities.

The Scenario

In 2024, SteelTrack Ltd. approached the consortium led by Pioneer Bank Ltd. for financial assistance of ₹422.66 crore to establish a steel manufacturing plant. The firm submitted a detailed project report along with detailed financial plans for project profitability. Pioneer Bank distributed the sanctioned credit facilities as follows:

Facility	Amount Sanctioned (₹ in Crores)
CAPEX/Term Loan (Plant Setup)	50.23
Cash Credit (Pre/Post WC)	18.62
Packing Credit (Sub-limit)	(5.10)
Import LC	195.78
Bank Guarantee (BG)	88.34

Supplier's Credit	42.56
Forward Exchange	6.80
Export Credit	25.43
Total	**422.66**

Initial stages of the project seemed promising, with procurement orders placed for machinery and construction activities underway. But, the company started defaulting on payments including term loan installments, cash credit obligations and BG obligations. An extensive probe revealed serious financial irregularities.

Problem Statement

SteelTrack Ltd. did not repay, resulting in several other financial and operational challenges coming to the fore:

a) **Non-repayment of Loans**: Term loans, export credit, and supplier's credit payments were irregular.

b) **Diversion of Funds**: ₹378.12 crore was sent to subsidiaries in places like Singapore, Hong Kong, Kenya and the UAE.

c) **Misuse of Facilities**:

   – BGs were invoked frequently, with delayed settlements.
   – Import letters of credits were issued for suspicious transactions without genuine underlying trade.

d) **Operational Failures**: The factory couldn't function properly due to technical breakdowns, leading to project delays & affecting cash flow.

The resulting financial stress posed significant risks for the consortium banks & underscored a lack of proper due diligence & monitoring.

Detailed Analysis

Observations and Lapses

Investigations uncovered several red flags like:

a) **Accommodation Bills**: SteelTrack Ltd. used to issue these accommodation bills to inflate the transaction volume and hide the diversion of funds.

b) **Unexplained Fund Transfers**: Large payments were made through shell companies and foreign subsidiaries with little or no operations.

c) **Lack of Physical Verification**: Machinery financed under the CAPEX loan was either not delivered or heavily overvalued.

d) **Frequent Invocation of BGs**: Multiple BGs were invoked, often due to non-performance of contracts, & payments were delayed, damaging the consortium's reputation.

e) **Irregular LC Transactions**: Documents under Import LCs were regularly dated on or before date of issue, indicating pre-agreement; implying non-genuine trade

f) **Non-disclosure of Relationships**: SteelTrack Ltd. maintained otherwise undisclosed banking relationships with non-consortium banks which were in violation of consortium norms.

g) **Ignored Alerts**: The branch staff do not check alerts from the bank's systems for exceptional transactions.

Fund Diversion Breakdown(Total Diversion : ₹378.12 Crores)

a) Singapore, Amount transferred ₹87.34 Crores (23.1%)

b) Hong Kong, Amount transferred ₹68.21 Crores (18.0%)

c) Kenya, Amount transferred ₹49.47 Crores (13.1%)

d) UAE, Amount transferred ₹92.78 Crores (24.5%)

e) Malaysia, Amount transferred ₹42.12 Crores (11.1%)

f) Indonesia, Amount transferred ₹38.20 Crores (10.2%)

(Percentage shows Percentage of Total Diversion)

Only 3 percent of the money that was diverted was traced back to actual businesses.

Solution and Resolution

Corrective Actions Taken

1) Forensic Audit & Legal Action

a) Forensic audit to the extent of ₹378.12 crores was done to trace the diversion of funds through shell companies.

b) Seizure of Assets: Assets of SteelTrack Ltd. and its promoters were confiscated under the SARFAESI Act, 2002 for loan recovery.

c) IBC Proceedings: The company was referred to the Insolvency and Bankruptcy Code (IBC), 2016, initiating corporate insolvency resolution.

d) Criminal Action: Promoters were booked under the Prevention of Money Laundering Act (PMLA), 2002, & legal cases were initiated.

e) Inter-bank Coordination: The Central Fraud Registry (CFR) was informed of the fraud to prevent promoters from obtaining any other banking facilities.

2) Strengthening Consortium Coordination

a) **Mandatory Consortium Meetings:** Monthly review meetings were prescribed for all participating banks to monitor loan accounts.

b) **Real-time Fund Utilization Tracking:** Consortium banks implemented a common platform to track fund movements & credit utilization.

c) **Inter-Bank Information Sharing:** Red-flagged transactions (large fund movements, multiple LCs, frequent BG invocations) were shared across banks to detect misuse.

3) Fraud Prevention and Improved Credit Monitoring

a) **AI-Powered Risk Alerts:** AI-based transaction monitoring was introduced to detect accommodation bills, irregular LC transaction & frequent invocation of BGs.

b) **Third-Party Asset Verification:** A third-party auditor was hired to physically verify the machinery acquisition under the CAPEX loan and prevent fictitious claims.

c) **Background Check on Associated Companies:** All entities concerned would be subjected to a strict KYC and forensic analysis to ensure that there is no siphoning of funds through shell firms.

4) Rectifying Lapses in Guarantees and Letter of Credit (LC) Transactions

a) For Bank Guarantees (BGs):

– Unsecured guarantees were prohibited, & limits were imposed on BGs issued per borrower.

– Strict exposure norms were maintained so that no single borrower had undue concentration in BG facilities.

– The pre-sanction due diligence was augmented to ascertain if the company would be able to honour BG obligations before it is issued.

b) For Letter of Credit (LCs):

- Banks started implementing stricter checks on LC transactions to see that all import documents match genuine trade transactions.
- Alerts generated by the system were implemented for all LC transactions above exposure limits and for new overseas parties.
- Bills under LCs were verified to ensure they were not pre-arranged frauds (i.e., dating on the next day of LC issue).

5) Strengthening Internal Bank Controls

a) Automated Early Warning Systems (EWS): Real-time monitoring of:

- BG invocation patterns
- LC usage trends
- Unusual cash credit utilization
- Irregular foreign remittances

b) Pre-disbursement Inspection: Physical verification of CAPEX-financed machinery was made mandatory.

c) Accountability of Bank Officials: Strict penalties and disciplinary action was imposed for any negligence in detecting fraud.

Key Learnings for Bankers

1) **Early Detection is Key:** An early identification of the red flags, irregular fund transfer as well as accommodation bills, helps in preventing escalation
2) **Strengthen Consortium Coordination:** Members of consortium banks should share information openly and act quickly to irregularities
3) **Comprehensive Monitoring Tools:** Using technology like Artificial Intelligence based transaction monitoring systems helps identify fraud in real-time.

Conclusion

The case of SteelTrack Ltd. underscores the dangers of lax credit monitoring & regulatory non-compliance in consortium banking. By implementing robust oversight mechanisms, adhering to regulatory norms, & utilizing advanced monitoring tools, banks can mitigate such risks and safeguard their financial health. This case will teach bankers the importance of vigilance, coordination & responsibility at all levels of the banking process.

* * *

CASE STUDY 35

COMPREHENSIVE CREDIT APPRAISAL: A CASE STUDY OF KALINGA PRECISION WORKS

Introduction

By January 2024, when the financial year-end was just around the corner, Mr. Rajeev Nayak, the branch manager of Konark Commercial Bank's branch at Bhubaneshwar, was busy thinking of ways & means to meet his targets for lending to MSMEs. A major thrust area was the Pradhan Mantri MUDRA Yojana (PMMY) which supports micro & small enterprises. During the course of the day, an application from Kalinga Precision Works (KP Works), a small-scale manufacturing unit in the outskirts of Bhubaneswar, emerged as a pivotal case.

KP Works required funding of ₹10,03,450 to buy CNC Wire-Cut Electrical Discharge Machine (EDM) for its expansion. The decision to approve the loan hinged on a thorough risk evaluation process & alignment with regulatory frameworks.

The Scenario

Kalinga Precision Works

KP Works, a Bhubaneswar-based MSME, was launched in 2022 by Mr. Aditya Das, who is 43 years of age & has sixteen years of experience in precision machining. Mr. Das operates the unit from a leased industrial shed located in Khurda Industrial Estate, Bhubaneswar. The company manufactured complex parts according to customers' needs with the help of CNC machines.

Proposed Machinery

KP Works recognised the DK-7735-M-LM CNC wire-cut EDM as an important asset priced at ₹10,03,450 (inclusive of GST & installation charges), the machine offered features such as high-speed multi-cut capability, robust control systems, & superior surface finishing. Acquisition was essential for the firm to improve productivity & bag high-value opportunities.

Projected Financials

The enterprise showcased forecasts that showed big growth:

a) **FY 2024 (Estimated):** Gross sales are projected at ₹3,18,750, with a net profit of ₹37,200, and net worth reaching ₹3,68,500.

b) **FY 2025:** A substantial increase is expected, with gross sales rising to ₹18,12,550, net profit increasing to ₹1,65,300, and net worth growing to ₹6,85,700.

c) **FY 2026:** Continued growth is forecasted, with gross sales climbing to ₹22,48,450, net profit soaring to ₹4,21,700, and net worth reaching ₹9,58,100.

d) **FY 2027:** The business anticipates achieving gross sales of ₹28,31,200, net profit of ₹6,84,400, and a net worth of ₹11,93,500.

Banking Relationship and Credit History

Mr. Das was a loyal customer of Konark Commercial Bank for the past six years. His flawless repayment record on consumer and gold loans, along with a good CIBIL score of 774, reflected a good credit profile.

Market Context

The need for CNC machining services in Odisha was increasing due to more machines getting installed as a part of industrial automation & MSME sector growth. KP Works, strategically located in a burgeoning industrial hub, was well-positioned to capitalize on this demand.

Problem Statement

The critical question was whether Konark Commercial Bank should approve the ₹10,03,450 term loan for KP Works under PMMY, considering the absence of traditional collateral, the borrower's strong credit history, & the potential risks inherent to a growing MSME.

Detailed Analysis

1) Credit Risk Scoring

The bank's credit scoring model assigned weighted scores on the demographic risk, business risk, financial risk & management risk.

a) Demographic Risk (Weightage: 20%)

- **Age:** At 43, Mr. Das earned 8/10.
- **Educational Qualification:** His ITI diploma secured 6/15.
- **Stability of Residence:** A decade-long stay in Bhubaneswar awarded 20/20.
- **Dependents:** One dependent resulted in a score of 7/10.

Total Score: 41/55.

b) Business Risk (Weightage: 30%)

- **Demand:** High demand for CNC machining services earned full marks (25/25).
- **Competition:** Moderate competition reduced the score to 10/20.
- **Supply Chain:** Proximity to suppliers and low raw materials delays secured (15/15).

Total Score: 50/60.

c) Financial Risk (Weightage: 30%)

- **Loan-to-Value Ratio (LTV):** At 1.02, this ratio earned 18/25.
- **Debt Service Coverage Ratio (DSCR):** Projected at 2.3, it received full marks (25/25).
- **TOL/TNW:** A ratio of 2.1 secured 8/10.

Total Score: 51/60.

d) Management Risk (Weightage: 20%)

- **Experience:** With 16 years of relevant experience, Mr. Das earned 20/25.
- **CIBIL Score:** Above 750, awarded the maximum 35/35.
- **Digital Transactions:** Providing digital payment options at very low fees - 9/15.

Total Score: 64/75.

2) Risk Grading

Using the weighted average formula:

Weighted Score = (Demographic Risk × 20%) + (Business Risk × 30%) + (Financial Risk × 30%) + (Management Risk × 20%)

KP Works was assigned a calculated weighted score of 81.4 which puts it under the risk category of SVL-2(Normal risk) which means it is satisfactory.

3) Collateral and CGFMU

RBI guidelines prohibit collateral for loans under ₹10 lakh to microenterprises. Instead, KP Works qualified for the Credit Guarantee Fund for Micro Units (CGFMU), which would guarantee 75% of the loan amount, leaving ₹2,50,862.5 as the bank's effective exposure.

A one-time guarantee fee of ₹2,508 and an annual service fee of ₹3,012 were charged, significantly reducing the bank's net exposure:

Guaranteed Amount: ₹7,52,587.5 (75% of ₹10,03,450).

Effective Exposure for Bank: ₹2,50,862.5.

4) Financial Viability

a) Break-Even Point: With annual fixed costs of ₹2,85,750 (or ₹23,812.50 per month), KP Works will break even in 14 months with a gross margin of 35%.

The fixed & variable costs for KP Works were analyzed to determine the break-even point (BEP).

Fixed Costs: ₹2,85,750 annually (including rent, salaries, & machine maintenance).

Variable Costs: 65% of gross sales.

BEP Calculation:

BEP(Sales) = Fixed Cost/Gross Margin Ratio

= ₹2,85,750/0.35 = ₹8,16,429

b) Profitability Trend: Operating profit was expected to grow steadily showcasing prudent financial management

5) Industry Trends

India's precision machine tools industry has experienced a CAGR of 12.8% over the past five years, with the state of Odisha emerging as a regional hub of precision manufacturing. KP Works was likely to gain from this favourable momentum.

Solution

According to analysis above, the following loan terms were proposed:

Loan Amount: ₹10,03,450
Interest Rate: 11.5% per annum with quarterly rests.
Tenure: 5 years, with an EMI of ₹21,908.
Security: Covered under CGFMU.
Monitoring: Quarterly submission of financial reports & bi-annual site inspections.

Implementation Plan

To ensure effective utilization of the loan & mitigate risks, the following implementation plan was proposed:

1) Loan Disbursement: Funds to be directly transferred to Eastern Tech Machines for the CNC machine purchase.

2) Monitoring Mechanism:

a)   Quarterly submission of financial statements.
b)   Biannual site inspections by the bank's credit team.

3) Performance Reviews: Annual comparison of projected vs. actual financial performance to identify variances & take corrective measures if necessary.

4) Customer Relationship Management: Strengthening the bank's relationship with KP Works by offering advisory services for operational improvements & cash flow management.

Outcome

Post loan disbursement in February 2024, KP Works quickly bought & installed the CNC machine. The impact on the business was tangible:

1)   **Increased Efficiency:** The new machine shortened the production lead time by 18%, thus orders were completed faster.
2)   **Expanded Clientele:** In the first six months, three new contracts added ₹2,75,450 of new revenue to KP Works.

3) **Improved Profit Margins:** The operating profit margins went up from 12.2 percent in FY 2024 to 18.4 percent in FY 2025.

By FY 2025, gross sales reached ₹18,72,350, slightly exceeding projections, & net profits rose to ₹1,72,800.

Key Takeaways for Bankers

1) **Robust Credit Assessment Framework:** The structured risk scoring of the bank helped balance risks and rewards for better lending of approvals.
2) **Leveraging Credit Guarantee Mechanisms:** The CGFMU scheme was very useful for funding for KP Works without additional security. This shows the importance of Government-led schemes.
3) **Proactive Loan Monitoring:** Regular reviews & inspections prevented the risk of misuse of the loan & assisted in adhering to the projected business plan.

* * *

CASE STUDY 36

Beyond the Balance Sheet: Financing a Multi-Sector Business in an Uncertain Economy

Introduction

Ms. Kavya Iyer, a seasoned corporate banker & head of JK Bank Ltd.'s regional office in Hubballi, Karnataka, faced a significant challenge when Nexus Chemicals & Textiles Ltd. (Nexus Ltd.) approached her for the renewal of its working capital facilities. Nexus Ltd., a long-time client of JK Bank Ltd., operates in two demanding sectors: chemical manufacturing & textile trading. As the leader of a 12-bank consortium, JK Bank Ltd. had to conduct a comprehensive credit analysis & present a well-structured recommendation to the consortium members and the bank's head office.

The company requested ₹2,153.47 crore in working capital facilities for FY 2024–25, citing its ambitious plans to scale operations, improve product offerings, and explore export opportunities in South Asia and the Middle East. Nexus Ltd is a dual-industry company that faces challenges such as different risk profiles, seasonality issues and widely differing working capital cycles.

The Scenario

Company Overview

Nexus Chemicals & Textiles Ltd. was founded in 1989 by Mr. Raghavendra Patil and is a well-known entity in the interior regions of Karnataka and has its headquarters at Dharwad. The company operates in two main divisions:

a) **Chemical Manufacturing Division:** Located in Belagavi, this division specializes in producing specialty chemicals, including adhesives, coatings, & industrial solvents. Nexus has invested heavily in research & development (R&D), enabling it to offer value-added products customized to client needs.

180

b) **Textile Trading Division:** With operations centered in Davangere, this division sources textiles such as cotton fabrics, synthetic blends, & technical textiles from both domestic & international markets for trading.

The company's commitment to sustainability is evident in its adoption of green chemistry principles & its use of renewable energy sources. Nexus runs a solar facility that provides 60 per cent of its energy needs & decreases dependence on conventional power.

Financial Performance

For FY 2023–24, Nexus Ltd. reported:

a) Net Sales: ₹4,713.62 crore, a 12.8% increase from the previous year.

- **Chemicals Division Revenue:** ₹2,905.49 crore (61.6% of total revenue).
- **Textiles Division Revenue:** ₹1,808.13 crore (38.4% of total revenue).

b) Export Revenue: ₹913.76 crore (19.4% of total sales).

c) Profit Before Tax (PBT): PBT was ₹76.58 crore, reflecting a modest profit margin.

d) Net Worth: ₹462.87 crore on total assets of ₹1,942.63 crore.

e) Foreign Currency Expenses: ₹1,437.22 crore, attributed to raw material imports & international textile procurement.

Problem Statement

Nexus Ltd. sought ₹2,153.47 crore in working capital facilities which were distributed as follows:

a) **Cash Credit:** 340.78 crore for liquidity management of both divisions
b) **Letters of Credit (LC):** ₹1,287.29 crore for procuring raw materials & textiles.
c) **Bank Guarantees (BG):** ₹525.40 crore for bidding, procurement, & advance payments in both divisions.

Some major concerns of JK Bank Ltd. were:

a)   Should Nexus Ltd. receive the full working capital facilities requested?

b)   How should Nexus's dual-industry business model be evaluated to judge appropriate credit limits?

c)   What steps can be taken by JK Bank Ltd. to hedge the risk of foreign exchange exposure, seasonal demand, & commodity price fluctuations?

Detailed Analysis and Solution

1) Segmented Financial Analysis

A) Chemical Division:

a)   **Revenue Contribution:** ₹2,905.49 crore in FY 2023–24.

b)   **Working Capital Cycle:** The division's cycle averages 180 days due to extended production times & storage requirements for specialty chemicals. Imported raw materials like polymers, solvents and additives account for an annual cost of ₹924.57 crore.

c)   **Operational Risk:** The chemical manufacturing industry is exposed to regulatory risk that may arise from the provisions of the Environmental Protection Act, 1986 and the Factories Act, 1948. All this can impact operations & production costs.

B) Textile Division:

a)   **Revenue Contribution:** ₹1,808.13 crore in FY 2023–24.

b)   **Working Capital Cycle:** With shorter lead times of 120 days, this division's needs are more immediate but subject to higher market volatility. Imported textiles account for ₹512.65 crore of annual procurement costs.

c)   **Market Volatility:** Currency exchange risks & geo-political elements affect import pricing & supply chain stability.

2) Credit Risk Evaluation

Credit ratings for FY 2023–24 revealed:

a)   **Short-term Facilities:** A2 (moderate risk).

b)   **Long-term Facilities:** BBB+ (stable outlook but above-average volatility).

Even though Nexus was continuously making profits, heavy dependence on imports and changing price of commodities involved a huge financial risk, which called for cautious approach.

3) Working Capital Calculation & Allocation

JK Bank Ltd. employed two fundamental techniques for working capital requirement assessment:

a) **Operating Cycle Method:** Focuses on the time taken to convert raw materials into cash. This consists of finding the working capital cycle (inventory days + receivables days – payable days).

b) **Projected Turnover Method:** Allocates working capital as a percentage of projected turnover for each division, considering the nature of operations, seasonality, & financial risks.

Cash Credit Allocation

Cash Credit is primarily needed to fund day-to-day operations, including inventory & receivables.

Formula: Cash Credit Requirement =

(Inventory Days + Receivables Days - Payables Days) x Projected Turnover/365

Inputs for Chemicals Division:

Projected Turnover (Chemicals): ₹2,905.49 crore

Inventory Days (Chemicals): 60 days

Receivables Days (Chemicals): 90 days

Payables Days (Chemicals): 45 days

Operating Cycle (Chemicals) : 60 + 90 – 45 = 105 days

Cash Credit Requirement (Chemicals) =105 / 365 x 2,905.49 = ₹ 210.56 crore

Inputs for Textiles Division:

Projected Turnover (Textiles): ₹1,808.13 crore

Inventory Days (Textiles): 45 days

Receivables Days (Textiles): 120 days

Payables Days (Textiles): 30 days

Operating Cycle (Textiles) : 45 + 120 − 30 = 135 days

Cash Credit Requirement (Textiles) = 135/365 x 1,808.13 = ₹ 130.22 crore

Total Cash Credit Allocation:

Total Cash Credit = ₹210.56 (Chemicals) + ₹130.22 (Textiles) = ₹340.78 crore

4) LC Limits Allocation

Both divisions require Letters of Credit (LC) for the procurement of raw materials.

Formula:

LC Requirement = Percentage of Imports under LC × Projected Raw Material Costs

Inputs for Chemicals Division:

a) Raw Material Costs (Chemicals): ₹2,213.12 crore

b) Percentage of Raw Materials Under LC (Chemicals): 75%

LC Requirement (Chemicals) = 0.75 × 2,213.12 = ₹1,659.84 crore

Since 50% of LCs are already self-funded through internal accruals:

LC Allocation (Chemicals) = 50% × ₹1,659.84 = ₹850.93 crore

Inputs for Textiles Division:

a) Raw Material Costs (Textiles): ₹1,324.76 crore

b) Percentage of Raw Materials Under LC (Textiles): 70%

LC Requirement (Textiles) 0.7 × 1,324.76 = ₹927.33 crore

With similar internal accrual funding of 50%:

LC Allocation (Textiles) = 50% × ₹927.33 = ₹436.36 crore

Total LC Allocation:

Total LC Limits = ₹850.93 (Chemicals) + ₹436.36(Textiles) = ₹1,287.29 crore

5) Bank Guarantee Allocation

Bank Guarantees (BG) are required for performance guarantees, advance payments, & procurement agreements.

Formula:

BG Allocation = Percentage of Contracts Requiring BGs × Contract Value

Inputs for Chemicals Division:

a) Total Contracts (Chemicals): ₹1,152.90 crore

b) Percentage of Contracts Requiring BGs (Chemicals): 30%

BG Requirement (Chemicals) = 0.3 × 1, 152.90 = ₹345.87 crore

Inputs for Textiles Division:

a) Total Contracts (Textiles): ₹598.43 crore

b) Percentage of Contracts Requiring BGs (Textiles): 30%

BG Requirement (Textiles) = 0.3 × 598.43 = ₹179.53 crore

Total BG Allocation:

Total BG Limits = ₹345.87 (Chemicals) + ₹179.53 (Textiles) = ₹525.40 crore

The Final Allocations Summary:

The allocation of financial facilities between the Chemicals Division and Textiles Division, totaling ₹2,153.47 crore across three key categories are :

a) **Cash Credit:** A total of ₹340.78 crore was allocated, with ₹210.56 crore assigned to the Chemicals Division and ₹130.22 crore to the Textiles Division.

b) **LC Limits:** The highest allocation was in Letter of Credit (LC) Limits, totaling ₹1,287.29 crore. The Chemicals Division received ₹850.93 crore, while the Textiles Division was allocated ₹436.36 crore.

c) **Bank Guarantees:** A total of ₹525.40 crore was allocated under bank guarantees, with ₹345.87 crore for the Chemicals Division and ₹179.53 crore for the Textiles Division.

The total allocation for the Chemicals Division amounts to ₹1,407.36 crore, whereas the Textiles Division received ₹746.11 crore. This distribution highlights a higher allocation to the Chemicals Division, particularly in LC Limits and Bank Guarantees, reflecting its greater need for credit and trade finance facilities.

6) Risk Mitigation Measures

To safeguard against financial & operational risks, JK Bank Ltd. proposed:

a) **Currency Hedging:** Nexus must hedge 80% of foreign exchange transactions exceeding ₹25 crore.

b) **Enhanced Collateralization:** Nexus promised more collateral like fixed assets worth ₹310 crore and also promoters' personal guarantees.

c) **Monitoring Mechanisms:** Monthly reviews of cash flow statements, inventory levels, & LC utilization to detect and address anomalies.

7) Methodology for Evaluation

JK Bank Ltd. makes use of a detailed cash flow analysis to assess season-wise demand patterns in both divisions. While chemical sales peaked during Q2 & Q3 due to industrial demand, textile sales surged during festive seasons, indicating the need for flexible credit limits.

Decision

Analyzing the situation, JK Bank Ltd. approved working capital facilities to the tune of ₹2,045.32 crore lower than what was requested. Stricter terms were imposed, including:

a) **Forex Hedging:** Compulsory hedging for all import transactions.

b) **Inventory Monitoring:** Quarterly audits to track inventory turnover & reduce obsolescence.

c) **Risk Sharing:** The consortium created a contingency fund of ₹50 crore for any untoward incident.

Key Learnings for Bankers

a) **Customized Credit Assessment:** Dual-industry companies require separate risk evaluations for each business segment, considering unique cycles, demand patterns, & risks.

b)   **Risk Mitigation Tools:** Hedging and collateralization are vital to protect banks from forex volatility & market disruptions.

c)   **Consortium Collaboration:** Effective communication & mechanisms for sharing risks amongst the banks of the consortium are critical in supporting complex clients like Nexus Ltd.

By taking these steps, JK Bank Ltd. made sure the bank and Nexus Ltd. are financially stable for long term growth with minimum risk.

* * *

Sealed, Stamped, Secure: The Crucial Role of Document Registration in Immovable Property Transactions

Introduction

Document registration plays an integral role in establishing the legal sanctity of transactions involving immovable property. It ensures transparency, avoids disputes, & safeguards the interests of all parties involved. In India, this process is governed by the Registration Act, 1908 with specified timelines, procedure, & consequences. This case study focuses on a real case where, due to non-registration in time, the party suffered legal complications. It also gives detailed insights, examples & data to show the importance of adherence to registration norms.

The Scenario

Mr. Rajesh Gupta, a retired government officer residing in Mumbai, inherited a 7.85-acre agricultural property in his ancestral village in Uttar Pradesh. The land is valued at ₹84,37,530 as per the market rate of ₹10,75,000 per acre. The land was transferred to Mr. Gupta through a deed executed on May 15, 2023. As two of the family members (co-signatories to the deed) were in Dubai, execution was staggered, and the deed was signed in parts.

Mr. Gupta, unaware of the Registration Act's requirements, delayed presenting the deed for registration, assuming that possession and informal family consent sufficed to secure his ownership rights. Problems came up when his cousin, Mr.Anil Sharma, who had an older, unregistered agreement made on 20 March 2019, and asked for ₹2,000,000 as compensation for giving up his alleged rights. To make the matters worse for Mr. Gupta the revenue office refused to mutate the land in his name until the dispute over ownership was settled by law.

Problem Statement

What could Mr. Gupta have done differently to safeguard his legal rights? What role does document registration play in preventing such disputes, & how do the provisions of the Registration Act provide redressal mechanisms for cases of delayed or invalid registration?

Detailed Analysis

1) Legal Requirements Under the Registration Act, 1908

Mandatory Registration of Immovable Property Documents:

a) According to section 17(1) of the Act, a sale deed, transfer deed or a gift deed related to any immovable property worth more than ₹ 100, to be mandatorily registered. This ensures the document's admissibility as evidence in a court of law.

b) However, as per Section 17(2), documents like will documents do not necessarily require registration, allowing flexibility in specific personal matters.

Timelines for Registration:

a) As per Section 23 of the Indian Registration Act, 1908, any document (other than a will) must be presented for registration within four months of its execution date; that is, it must be submitted to the relevant registration office to be officially registered.

b) In cases where execution occurs abroad, registration must be completed within four months of the document's arrival in India.

Penalties for Delayed Registration:

According to section 25 of Registration Act, 1908, an extension of registration of a document, that has already delayed registration, may be given for a period not exceeding four months on justifiable reasons such as "urgent necessity" or "unavoidable accident" upon payment of fine will not exceed usually ten times the normal registration fee.

In short, The timeline for document registration consists of two phases:

a) **Initial Registration Period** – Documents must be registered within 4 months from execution. There is no penalty if completed within this timeframe.

b) **Extended Registration Period** – If the initial deadline is missed, an additional 4 months is allowed for registration, but with a fine. The penalty can be up to 10 times the registration fee.

2) Importance of Sub-Registrar's Jurisdiction

a) Documents must be registered in the Sub-Registrar's office of the district where the property is located as provided in Section 28. For Mr. Gupta's property, the Sub-Registrar's office at Bijnor, Uttar Pradesh had jurisdiction.

b) The Registrar may accept documents intended for subordinate offices but cannot override jurisdictional requirements without valid reasons.

3) Execution and Authentication (Section 58(1)(a))

a) The Act requires all parties who execute the document to be present before the Registrar for Identity verification and acknowledgment of execution.

b) If parties are unable to appear at the same time, staggered appearances may be permitted, but within time.

c) In the case of Mr. Gupta, his relatives staying in Dubai could have given power of attorney of its representative in India to register timely.

4) Practical Implications of Non-Registration

The unregistered document presented by Mr. Sharma highlights the risks associated with unregistered agreements. Under section 49 of the Registration Act, unregistered documents cannot be used as evidence in case of a dispute involving immovable property. Mr. Sharma's claim was therefore weak; because of this, the resolution process was delayed. As a result, Mr. Gupta incurred legal costs of ₹187,540 & was under stress for a few months.

Resolution

On understanding of the severity of the matter, Mr. Gupta took legal advice. His lawyer recommended the following course of action:

1) Immediate Registration with Penalty Payment:

a) The deed was presented to the Sub-Registrar in Bijnor on September 22, 2023, four months beyond the initial deadline.

b)   A penalty of ₹13,250 (5x the registration fee of ₹2,650) was imposed & paid to secure the document's registration.

2) Appearance of All Parties:

a)   Mr. Gupta talked to his relatives in Dubai who executed powers of attorney by appointing a local representative for acknowledgment before the Sub-Registrar.

b)   This allowed compliance with Section 58(1)(a) without being physically present.

3) Mutation in Revenue Records:

Once registered, the deed was submitted to the revenue department for mutation. After the verification of the registration details, the land records were updated by the department which made Mr. Gupta the sole owner.

Event	Date	Cost (₹)	Remarks
Deed Execution	May 15, 2023	-	Incomplete without registration
Deadline for Registration	September 15, 2023	-	Missed
Actual Registration Date	September 22, 2023	15,900	Includes fine and registration fee
Legal Fees (Dispute Resolution)	August–October 2023	1,87,540	Lawyer and procedural costs
Land Valuation	-	84,37,530	Based on market rate of ₹10,75,000/acre

Key Financials and TimelineKey Learnings for Bankers

1) Timely Documentation is Non-Negotiable:

The Bankers should ensure that all the documents, especially those which relate to collateral like immovable property are registered within the time limits prescribed. This avoids potential disputes & secures the bank's interests.

2) Guidance on Legal Provisions:

It is advisable to inform clients about sections 17(1), 23, and 49 of the Registration Act so that a misunderstanding does not occur & ownership is protected.

3) Proactive Risk Management:

It is the responsibility of banks to check whether the documents are genuine & registered before sanction of loan or other facilities. Regular training on evolving property laws ensures compliance & reduces risk exposure.

Conclusion

This case shows how important it is to register documents to show legality of property transactions. For bankers, it is a reminder to stay alert, counsel clients better & comply with laws. By proactively addressing documentation gaps, financial institutions can avoid prolonged disputes, minimize legal risks, & uphold the trust of their clients.

* * *

CASE STUDY 38

THE DOUBLE-EDGED SWORD: LOAN AGAINST BOOK DEBTS

Introduction

Book debts, a critical component of trade finance, represent outstanding receivables arising from credit sales. Businesses can get loans against these receivables to raise liquidity & banks get the lending opportunities. However, the practice of advancing loans against book debts comes with inherent risks, requiring meticulous due diligence & strict adherence to legal frameworks. This case study examines a real-life scenario involving City Union Bank and its client M/S Gupta Traders, highlighting how loans against book debts can be structured effectively, with the risks mitigated through robust checks and balances.

The Scenario

City Union Bank, a leading private sector bank in India, was approached by M/S Gupta Traders, a mid-sized enterprise dealing in electronic components. The company sought an overdraft facility of ₹82,43,750 against its book debts to finance its working capital requirements.

M/S Gupta Traders had an annual turnover of ₹12.73 crore, with receivables amounting to ₹2.54 crore at the time of application. Most of the receivables of ₹1.47 crore (57.87%) were from a single customer Global Mart Pvt. Ltd., a retail giant. Even though the borrower paid on time in the past, over-dependence on one client & delays in realisation of receivables leads to potential risks.

City Union Bank faced a critical decision: whether to extend credit while ensuring the bank's exposure remained within acceptable risk limits.

Problem Statement

How can City Union Bank offer an overdraft facility to M/S Gupta Traders secured against book debts with acceptable risks & regulatory requirements?

Detailed Analysis

1) Legal Framework and Assignment Process

City Union Bank proceeded under the provisions of **Section 130 of the Transfer of Property Act**, which permits the assignment of actionable claims, including receivables. The following measures were implemented to ensure compliance & create a valid charge over the book debts:

a) **Assignment Agreement**: A formal document - assignment agreement was executed between M/S Gupta Traders & City Union Bank transferring the rights over book debts to the bank.

b) **Notice to Debtors**: Written notices were sent to Global Mart Pvt. Ltd. & all other debtors of M/S Gupta Traders, informing them about the assignment.

c) **Charge Registration**: For additional security, the hypothecation of book debts was registered with the **Registrar of Companies** under the Companies Act, 2013.

2) Verification and Due Diligence

City Union Bank implemented a full authentication process analysing the quality & genuine of the receivables.

Age of Receivables:

The receivables were analysed to make sure that they are not older than six months. Approximately ₹1.89 crore (74.4%) of the total receivables met this criterion. However, receivables worth ₹37.25 lakh (14.6%) were flagged as overdue.

Debtor Concentration:

With 57.87% of the receivables linked to Global Mart Pvt. Ltd., the bank identified a significant concentration risk. To overcome this, City Union Bank decided to cap the drawing power so that not more than 40% of the facility was dependent upon the receivables from one single client.

Verification of Sales Invoices and Ledgers:

Invoices and ledgers of the debtors were examined to check that the receivables were for genuine trades. No discrepancies or fictitious accounts were detected.

Market Opinion on Global Mart Pvt. Ltd.:

Feedback from credit agencies & market sources confirmed that Global Mart Pvt. Ltd. had a stable financial standing thereby mitigating the risk of default.

3) Structuring the Facility

City Union Bank arranged the overdraft facility as follows based on the findings of the due diligence process:

Sanctioned Limit – The total sanctioned limit is ₹65,95,000, which accounts for 80% of verified receivables.

Margin – A 20% margin is required, ensuring risk coverage.

Interest Rate – The applicable interest rate is 9.75% per annum, which is a floating rate, subject to market changes.

Tenure – The facility is provided for 3 months, with the possibility of renewal upon review.

Maximum Drawing Power from Global Mart Pvt. Ltd. Receivables – The borrower can utilize up to ₹26,38,000, which constitutes 40% of the total sanctioned facility.

City Union Bank also mandated that all receivables must be routed through the loan account to ensure transparency & effective monitoring.

4) Risks and Mitigation

The bank identified & mitigated the following risks:

a) **Fictitious or Disputed Receivables**: Financing was done only for genuine receivables arising out of trade transactions after strict due diligence.
b) **Over-Dependence on a Single Debtor**: By capping the drawing power linked to Global Mart Pvt. Ltd. at ₹26,38,000, City Union Bank reduced the risk of over-reliance.
c) **Delays in Receivables Realization**: Borrower has to send weekly updates on the status of receivables & recovery efforts.

5) Compliance and Monitoring

To maintain smooth functioning & avoid future risks, City Union Bank put in place following measures:

a)   **Periodic Verification**: Sales ledgers & invoices were reviewed monthly to identify any new overdue debts.

b)   **Confirmation of Assignment**: All debtors acknowledged the assignment of receivables, confirming the amount of debt & any rights of set-off.

c)   **Borrower Undertaking**: M/S Gupta Traders provided an undertaking that all collections would be deposited into the overdraft account.

6) Financial Viability and Impact

The facility provided a much-needed liquidity boost to M/S Gupta Traders, enabling the company to manage its working capital efficiently. Over three months, ₹58,47,500 (88.7% of the outstanding facility) was repaid as receivables were realized. The bank earned ₹1,47,112 in interest income during this period.

Key Learnings for Bankers: Checklist for Bankers- Loan Against Book Debts

1)   **Proper Documentation for Assignment**: Ensure the assignment of book debts is in writing, signed by the transferor, & notified to the debtor as per Sec. 130 of the Transfer of Property Act.

2)   **Thorough Verification of Book Debts**: Verify sales invoices & debtor ledgers to assess overdue receivables, reasons for non-payment, and the possibility of recovery.

3)   **Assess Creditworthiness of Borrower & Debtors**: Conduct a detailed credit appraisal of the borrower & the debtors, ensuring the financial health & repayment capability of both.

4)   **Monitor Age & Quality of Book Debts**: It's preferable to have book debts not older than six months; some banks prefer only up to three months old.

5)   **Diversification of Receivables**: Do not finance book debts where most of the sales are to one buyer, as the default risk is high.

6)   **Scrutinize Nature of Transactions**: Make sure that the debts come from actual trading transactions and not from the firm's sister concerns or capital expenditures or synthetic advances.

7) **Security Charging Methodology:** Differentiate between assignment (bank gets direct claim) & hypothecation (bank has equitable charge), ensuring appropriate security structuring.

8) **Risks in Lending Against Receivables:** Watch for fictitious, disputed, or old accounts, as well as borrowers with poor financial integrity.

9) **Legal Compliance and ROC Registration:** When a company assigns book debts, the charge must be registered with the Registrar of Companies (ROC).

10) **Control Over Collections:** Obtain an undertaking from the borrower that any debt collected directly will be passed to the bank, ensuring proper credit control.

* * *

CASE STUDY 39

UNPACKING THE LEGAL, OPERATIONAL, AND ETHICAL COMPLEXITIES OF BANK GUARANTEE INVOCATION

The Scenario

A branch of State Bank issued a Bank Guarantee worth ₹50 lakhs in favour of the Oil Authority of India for its client, a construction company. The BG was valid for three years with an additional clause permitting the beneficiary to invoke it within 3 months after expiry. At the end of this period, the Oil Authority invoked the BG alleging a violation of the terms of the contract.

The construction company contested the invocation, arguing that it had completed the work without issue and alleging that Oil Authority officials had asked for bribes. They filed a suit in the court for an injunction alleging the invocation was false. The court rejected these allegations and stated that bank guarantees are irrevocable and binding except in the event of fraud, which is proved.

Deeper Dive: Legal, Operational, and Ethical Aspects

As the State Bank branch head, you will have to find a way around this incident keeping in mind the law, operational aspects and customer relations. It is quite important to know the principles of bank guarantees and apply them.

I) Bank Guarantee as a Financial Instrument

Section 126 of the Indian Contract Act 1872 defines a "contract of guarantee" as a contract in which one party promises to perform the obligation of the third party or pay money in case of default. This arrangement involves three parties.

1) Principal Debtor: The individual whose obligation or liability is guaranteed.

2) Creditor: The party to whom the guarantee is given.

3) Surety: The person who provides the guarantee.

The surety's liability is secondary and only arises on the default of the principal debtor. Notably, such a guarantee can be either oral or written.

Bank Guarantee in the given case is a tripartite contract involving:

1) **Guarantor (Surety):** State Bank, providing the BG.
2) **Principal Debtor:** The construction company.
3) **Creditor (Beneficiary):** Oil Authority of India.

Key Characteristics of Bank Guarantees

a) **Irrevocability:** The BG binds the bank to honour that claim without any conditions upon demand from the beneficiary, provided that the claim is within the terms of the agreement.
b) **Payability on Demand:** The courts have consistently been upholding the enforceability of BGs and granting injunctions only in case of fraud or damage being irretrievable in nature.

Judicial Precedent

Indian Courts including the SC have observed that BGs should act as an independent contract separated from the underlying contract between customer and beneficiary. This independence guarantees that banks meet their obligations without getting caught in contractual disputes.

II) Strategic Response to the Case

To address this complex situation effectively, the following multidimensional approach is required:

1) Legal Review of the Invocation

a) **Verification of Terms:** Check that the demand complies with the BG terms, time schedule and documentation. Make sure that the Oil Authority invoked the BG within the three-month constraint.
b) **Fraud Investigation:** Even if the court did not grant the customer's request, does the review of internal documents reveal signs of fraud or coercion?

2) Operational Compliance

a)   **Obligation to Pay:** The Bank must act promptly to pay the amount of invocation and honour its credibility as well as the law. If the bank fails to fulfill the BG, the State Bank may get sued or fined.

b)   **Escalation Mechanism:** Inform senior management about the customer's allegations against the beneficiary for discussion. If fraud is suspected, notify the authorities for an investigation.

3) Customer Engagement

c)   **Transparent Communication:** The bank is obligated to honour the BG and nothing more, communicate with the customer. Clearly outline the court's stance on their allegations.

d)   **Advisory Role:** Help the customer reduce the risk in future contracts by suggesting the customer insert stricter performance clauses and seek legal remedies upfront.

4) Ethical Considerations

a)   **Balancing Obligations:** A fulfillment of the BG is a legal mandate, but the complaint of malpractice by the beneficiary must be ethically monitored. An internal inquiry should be initiated to investigate any negligence on the part of the bank while issuing the BG.

b)   **Safeguarding Reputation:** Show the integrity of the bank by handling customer complaints fairly and within the regulations.

III) Operational Insights and Strategic Safeguards

1) Risk Mitigation at BG Issuance

a)   **Stringent Due Diligence:** Vet the customer's credentials and the project's feasibility thoroughly before issuing BGs.

b)   **Clauses to Minimize Ambiguities:** Include explicit invocation criteria to reduce potential disputes.

2) Strengthening Governance

a)   **Enhanced Monitoring Mechanisms:** Periodically review BGs issued by the branch to identify potential red flags.

b)   **Internal Training:** Equip staff with advanced knowledge of contractual obligations and risk management.

3) Conflict Resolution Framework

a) **Dedicated Mediation Channels:** Create mechanisms to resolve disagreements between consumers and beneficiaries without going to court.

b) **Regular Feedback Mechanisms:** Encourage consumers to proactively share concerns for a long-term relationship

Key Lessons for Bankers

a) **Adherence to Legal Obligations:** Always honor BGs unconditionally unless there is documented fraud or court orders explicitly permitting a deviation.

b) **Proactive Risk Management:** At the BG issuance stage, implement checks and balances to keep future liability to a minimum.

c) **Customer-Centric Approach:** Maintain customer advocacy while meeting your own regulatory and operational obligations to build trust.

* * *

Conclusion

Congratulations on completing this transformative journey through the insightful pages of "The Fearless Banker: Banking Case Studies and Rationale" Throughout this book, you've explored real-world banking scenarios designed not merely to educate, but to empower you. You have seen how practicing banking on the ground is very different from the theory you have been taught. Therefore, being prepared, having confidence and clarity will make you successful.

By actively engaging with the 39 practical case studies presented, you've sharpened your decision-making skills, mastered critical banking concepts, and learned to navigate even the most intricate operational challenges with assurance. You now understand precisely how to handle garnishee and attachment orders, complex nomination issues, intricate deceased account settlements, sensitive locker operations, & complex lending decisions involving fraudulent activities & misrepresented stock statements. Each case has provided actionable insights, common pitfalls, and strategic solutions—ensuring you're never left guessing again.

You've also gained insights on how to confidently tackle daily banking issues, reducing your dependency on inadequate or ambiguous guidance from senior management. By reflecting on these realistic scenarios, you've developed the ability to manage customer disputes, confidently address grievances, & execute complex credit appraisals with accuracy and authority. Your improved credit analysis capabilities and risk assessment skills mean fewer costly mistakes, protecting you from avoidable audits or disciplinary repercussions.

Beyond technical skills, this book also served as your mentor, preparing you for accelerated career progression. If you are currently working as an entry-level banker or possibly moving towards managerial or senior roles, the practical advice shared here has prepared you for the next level. It empowered you to take challenges head-on instead of being overwhelmed or anxious about new roles or complicated scenarios.

This book is designed not merely as a reference guide but as your personal mentor. It will continuously help you in your banking profession. It will empower you to grow into higher responsibilities confidently and establish credibility among colleagues & customers. Going through these cases again will help reinforce important lessons and discover new insights that keep you engaged and updated.

If you've ever felt anxious or uncertain in your banking career, let this book be the transformative resource that turns doubt into assurance, confusion into clarity, & ordinary banking experiences into extraordinary expertise. Equip yourself with practical, actionable knowledge to excel consistently, avoid costly errors, & prevent disciplinary actions.

As you close this book, let it mark not an end, but a new beginning. You're better prepared, more informed and more self-confident. Move forward with the confidence that you now have the knowledge & wisdom to deal with the modern world of banking proactively, ethically and effectively.

Welcome to your transformed banking career—a journey marked by capability, clarity, & unwavering confidence. Use these learnings in day-to-day banking, keep growing, & become the exceptional banker your customers trust and your boss admires.

Your journey towards becoming an exceptional banking professional starts here—**embrace it, excel in it, and rise fearlessly.**

About the Author

Kumar Gaurav Khullar is a seasoned banker, trade finance expert, and passionate educator with a wealth of experience in the financial sector. An ex-banker of Bank of India and Punjab & Sind Bank, he has served at urban and rural branches with hands-on experience in General Banking, Credit/Advances & Risk Management.

An accomplished academic, he holds an MBA from the prestigious Indian Institute of Management, Raipur (IIM-Raipur) and a Master's in Computer Applications (MCA) from the Centre for Development of Advanced Computing (CDAC-Noida). He is also a JAIIB & CAIIB certified professional from the Indian Institute of Banking and Finance, supplemented by specialized banking certifications from NIBSCOM (National Institute of Banking Studies & Corporate Management) & other premier financial institutions.

In 2018, he transitioned from banking services to teaching & content creation, driven by his mission to simplify complex financial concepts and make professional certifications more accessible to bankers. Since then, he has assisted numerous bankers and finance professionals in preparing for and being able to clear JAIIB, CAIIB, Certified Credit Professional (CCP), and Anti-Money Laundering (AML) & Trade Finance exams.

A popular instructor, he teaches many best-selling courses on Udemy. These include Basel Norms Masterclass and Incoterms 2020 Masterclass. His courses have received excellent feedback from students. He also runs the Bank Financial Management Case Studies course which is a case studies-based specialized course meant for banking/finance professionals.

Furthermore, he has a YouTube community of over 55,000+ members where he shares practical insights on banking, career options and survival strategies for bankers. His videos, such as *"Factoring and Forfeiting Masterclass, Important Points Before Taking Charge of a New Branch", Ultimate Guide to Loan Proposals, Documentation and NPA Prevention for Bank Officers and Managers & "Save Your Banking Job – Vigilance 24/7"*, have helped countless bankers navigate real-world banking challenges.

With a mission to empower bankers with knowledge and confidence, Kumar Gaurav Khullar continues to bridge the gap between theory & practical banking through his books, courses, and mentoring initiatives. His work is not limited to banking certifications preperations, but also transforming careers and the future of banking.

You can contact me at - **kumargauravkhullar1@gmail.com**